Y^{OUR} B^{ANK}

How to Get Better Service

YOUR BANK

How to Get Better Service

JEFF DAVIDSON
and the Editors of
Consumer Reports Books

CONSUMER REPORTS BOOKS

A DIVISION OF CONSUMERS UNION

Yonkers, New York

Library of Congress Cataloging-in-Publication Data

Davidson, Jeffrey P.
    Your bank: how to get better service / Jeff Davidson and the
editors of Consumer Reports Books.
        p.   cm.
    Includes index.
    ISBN 0-89043-402-6
    1. Banks and banking—Customer services. 2. Banks and banking.
I. Consumer Reports Books. II. Title.
HG1616.C87D38   1992
332.1′75—dc20   91-46347
                                                                     CIP

First printing, March 1992

Manufactured in the United States of America

Your Bank—How to Get Better Service is a Consumer Reports Book published
by Consumers Union, the nonprofit organization that publishes Consumer
Reports, the monthly magazine of test reports, product Ratings, and buying
guidance. Established in 1936, Consumers Union is chartered under the Not-
for-Profit Corporation Law of the State of New York.

The purposes of Consumers Union, as stated in its charter, are to provide
consumers with information and counsel on consumer goods and services, to
give information on all matters relating to the expenditure of the family income,
and to initiate and to cooperate with individual and group efforts seeking to create and maintain decent living standards.

Consumers Union derives its income solely from the sale of Consumer
Reports and other publications. In addition, expenses of occasional public service
efforts may be met, in part, by nonrestrictive, noncommercial contributions,
grants, and fees. Consumers Union accepts no advertising or product samples
and is not beholden in any way to any commercial interest. Its Ratings and
reports are solely for the use of the readers of its publications. Neither the Ratings, nor the reports, nor any Consumers Union publications, including this
book, may be used in advertising or for any commercial purpose. Consumers
Union will take all steps open to it to prevent such uses of its material, its name,
or the name of Consumer Reports.

To my parents,
    who started me off
    with a passbook savings account
    at the tender age of eight.

ACKNOWLEDGMENTS

I wish to acknowledge Deborah Finkel, William Cooke, Willis Shen, and Sharon Cavileer for their writing, researching, or editing assistance; Chuck Dean and Bill Adler for the conceptual support and encouragement; and Roslyn Siegel, Sarah Uman, Kathleen Anderson, and the other fine folks at Consumer Reports Books for their professionalism and service to consumers everywhere.

CONTENTS

PREFACE

REMEMBER THE GOOD OLD DAYS, WHEN THE BANK OFFICER YOU HAD known for years would handle everything from a personal loan to an overdrawn checking account to the financing on a major business expansion? What happened? Why has this type of banking relationship vanished? In part, it has happened because many small community banks across the United States were gobbled up by bigger banks. In addition, regulation, social changes, and technology have produced fundamental shifts in the role of the banking industry in American life.

It often seems that in recent years dealing with banks has become more costly and complex while the level of service and attention offered to individual accounts has declined. The increases in service charges and loan processing fees, for example, have become cause for concern among banking customers.

From monthly account fees and service charges to exorbitant closing costs for mortgages, things have changed to the point that it's not uncommon for consumers to feel that they are being exploited. In fact, many people who believe that they're being taken advantage of by their banks are actually right. Despite attractive advertisements that attempt to persuade people that banks are concentrating their efforts on making money for customers, one needs to remember that the primary purpose of banks is to make money for themselves.

Unless they are executing some short-term marketing plans, banks try to offer the lowest rates on passbook savings, money market accounts, and certificates of deposit that will still bring in funds. As well as minimizing the amounts they pay out, banks attempt to maximize the amounts they collect, charging customers for everything possible, including checking accounts, automated teller transactions, personalized checks, money orders, and checking accounts that fall below a minimum balance, all in addition to the money they make simply by keeping yours on deposit.

Yet there are methods you can employ to help get your bank to treat you and your money as among the bank's most important assets—which they are. Consider trying to get a loan. Though banks need to write loans, they often seem tight with available funds. Without interest income from loans and investment income from customer deposits, banks would cease to exist—all bankers know this.

Few people are aware that they have this leverage as bank customers, and that it can be used to get them better rates and service. The customer who is cognizant of this and is equipped to shop wisely is more apt to get a loan and at a lower rate.

This book won't bog you down with complicated formulas or charts. But if you suspect that you are not making use of the valuable services you can get from a bank, read on to determine ways to save money, make wise deposits, and gain a more favorable position when dealing with your bank.

Your Bank
How to Get Better Service

Introduction: The Bank in Today's Environment

ROBERT LOUIS STEVENSON ONCE SAID, "EVERYBODY LIVES BY selling something." This is no less true of bankers. They want to sell you their products and services. With proper knowledge, you can make today's new banking environment work better for you.

Unlike in years past, financial institutions now actively compete for consumer business. Glance through the advertising splashed throughout the pages of your newspaper's business section and there is little room for doubt.

Why the sudden interest? As commercial lending gets riskier in a volatile economic environment, and as bank deregulation has pushed the industry to a new level of competition, banks are looking at the "retail," or consumer, side of the business for new customers.

☐ BANKS IN A REGULATED ENVIRONMENT

Prior to deregulation in the eighties, there was only a limited amount of direct competition among banks for consumer deposits. The maximum interest rate paid on savings accounts was regulated by the government and banks were prohibited from paying interest on checking accounts.

In this climate banks did not vie for your savings. They simply sat back and waited on those people who happened to walk through the door. Usually, consumers selected their banks based solely on location: The nearest bank won.

According to Martin Mayer, author of *The Bankers*, prior to deregulation, bankers kept bankers' hours, delayed the availability of funds, and dealt with both depositors and borrowers in a lordly, if lazy, way. They had neither interest in nor talent for redesigning their services to meet the wishes of users. They had a monopoly.

□   ## THE EIGHTIES—THE DECADE OF DEREGULATION AND CHANGE

In the late seventies, many consumers began to shift their savings from bank accounts to money market mutual funds to earn higher yields. This alarmed the banking industry, which saw mutual funds as a threat to its own survival.

In response, banks asked Congress to eliminate the interest rate ceilings and other restrictions that prevented them from paying competitive rates on deposit accounts. Congress agreed. In 1980, it passed a law that phased out almost all interest rate restrictions on deposit accounts over a six-year timetable. By 1986, interest rates on savings accounts, CDs, and interest-bearing checking accounts were set by bank policy, not federal law.

Deregulation of the deposit side of banking affected the industry's lending activities. Because banks were paying more to borrow funds from their depositors, they were forced to charge their borrowers higher fees and interest rates. Because their interest costs on deposit accounts fluctuated with market interest rates, banks and savings-and-loans turned more and more to variable-rate mortgages and other variable-rate loan products. With variable-rate loans, banks can more readily match their interest earnings with their interest costs.

Aside from deposit account deregulation, dramatic geographic deregulation of the banking industry occurred during the last decade. Prior to the eighties, most banks operated exclusively within the boundaries of one state. Banks could expand into a new state only if the law of that state permitted it.

At the beginning of the decade, only one state permitted interstate banking. Today, only Montana and Hawaii prohibit it.

Many of the nation's largest banks hit the ground running when the old restrictions against interstate banking were lifted. As the decade wore on, their expansion dreams were made easier by the record number of bank and savings-and-loan insolvencies. They could enter a new market by acquiring a "dead" institution—often at rock bottom prices. The federal government, as receiver, was more than happy to find a ready and willing purchaser.

Other forces also changed the face of banking in the eighties. For example, hoping to cut teller costs, banks invested heavily in automated teller machines (ATMs) and ATM networks. Banking became more convenient but less personal.

Increasingly, as their Third World loans turned sour and their traditional corporate customers turned to alternative finanacial sources, many banks turned to consumer and mortgage lending for profits. Savings-and-loans turned to high-rise real estate development loans and investments to supplement their traditional home mortgage lending.

Deregulation, inevitably, and perhaps irrevocably, changed the banking industry. For the uninformed, deregulation has meant mass confusion. The lines distinguishing banks, savings-and-loans, credit unions, and brokerage firms have been blurred. Today, your broker offers you a checking account, while your bank can set up brokerage services for you. Banks may advertise high rates on CDs but then tack on an additional charge per month to maintain your checking account. One bank offers a home equity line of credit without any closing costs, while another charges closing costs but offers a lower interest rate.

Without question, banks are battling for upscale customers. These consumers are now in a relative position of strength and can "sell" (actually rent) their money to whichever bank pays the most interest on their accounts. But consumers with average or below average incomes can and often do pay a price for the negative side of deregulation. For example, before deregulation banks rarely imposed fees on deposit accounts because their interest costs were so low. Now service fees are common. Banks impose most of these fees on those customers with the lowest balances, allowing upscale consumers to earn market rates and avoid all fees.

There have been other problems associated with deregulation. With both higher interest rates and higher fees on savings and a broad array of credit products and prices, deregulation has forced consumers to educate themselves about the world of banking to obtain good banking services at the best price. Also, in an ever-increasing effort to win deposit dollars, banks have paid out higher and higher rates to depositors and have invested new funds in increasingly risky ventures in the hope of earning enough money to cover the higher payouts. A predictable result has been higher numbers of bank failures.

☐ THE NEED FOR KNOWLEDGE

Every week we read about "troubled" financial institutions and hear about failed banks on the evening news. New banks spring up in every shopping center while old downtown banks are acquired by mega-banks or merge with another financial group. Names and logos change. We worry about the safety of our deposited funds. To the average consumer, it's a nightmare.

Deregulation, increased competition, and a volatile economy have created a new financial services industry, however. Through knowledge you can help make this new world of banking work for you.

Secrets About Banks, or What the Banking Industry Will Never Tell You

---

S INCE THE MID-EIGHTIES, MOST OF THE NEWS COVERAGE REGARD-
ing the financial services industry has reflected bad news.
In 1988, an average of 4 banks a week closed their doors. About
1 bank in 65 now fails each year.

Many of the factors that converged to precipitate the banking
crisis—a volatile real estate market, regional recessions, and bad
loans to Third World countries, as well as deregulation, junk
bonds, and poor judgment in risk management—still have a
strong impact on the industry. The continued reports of bank failure resulting from faulty loan administration and fraud have badly
eroded consumer confidence in banks and in the entire financial
services industry.

Partly as a result of the growing turmoil, and partly because of
entrenched banking attitudes, most banks work hard to keep
information about themselves from becoming public knowledge.
Beyond the S&L crisis and all the headlines, however, are secrets
about banks you need to know.

Every industry has its problems. All things considered, banking is probably near the top of the list of industries experiencing bedlam. By some estimates, 75 percent of bank failures are directly or indirectly caused by the professional failure of bank officers or administrative staff. In Texas, for example, hundreds of multi-million-dollar loan packages were made by banks accepting false financial statements and false appraisals.

❑   **THE RISE OF BANK FRAUD**

Despite investigation by the government and the focus of the press on industry failures, bank fraud is a widespread problem. Industry experts say that computerization has made it easier than ever to engage in fraudulent schemes, and indeed, the number of frauds perpetrated each year and the dollar amount lost per incident is rising.

Today industry losses to internal bank fraud easily exceed losses to bank robbery. *Banker's Magazine* reported in its July 1990 issue that fraud contributes to unprecedented losses, which in turn prompt banks to increase service fees. The FBI's annual crime rate statistics reveal that in 1988 the agency investigated slightly fewer than 7,000 bank robbery incidents totaling nearly $47 million in losses, with an average loss per robbery of $6,700. In contrast, during that same year, the FBI investigated more than 17,000 incidents of bank fraud, totaling more than $2 billion in losses, with an average loss per incident of $128,496. What's worse, each year for the last three years bank fraud losses have doubled, and these figures reflect *only those cases reported and investigated.* They do not represent total industry losses, which likely add up to several hundred billion dollars.

Massive incidents of insider fraud result in your paying higher fees on all bank services so the bank can continue to show a profit. In addition, you pay for bank fraud through your taxes—for FBI investigations, court proceedings, bailing out the savings-and-loan institutions, and so forth. Given the realities within the industry, loss of confidence in banking on the part of the consumer is not surprising.

❏ EXCESSIVE EARNINGS AT THE TOP, PAUPER WAGES AT THE BOTTOM

Despite the industry's less than dazzling record, over the past decade, bank officers' salaries have climbed steadily. The compensation received by top banking executives often matches or exceeds what is earned by top executives in other industries.

The chief executive officer and top officers in the largest banks in the United States receive from $500,000 to $1,500,000 or more in total annual compensation. Even in your hometown bank, the CEO's base salary probably ranges from $185,000 to $285,000, with added bonuses and capital accumulations. Other operating officers and senior managers receive a base salary ranging from $80,000 to $140,000, depending on their title and bank location.

In many instances, bankers receive bonus and benefit packages equal to 30 to 50 percent *or more* of their published salaries. Such compensation can be effectively shielded from shareholders.

Exorbitant salaries and benefits, however, are enjoyed only by those at the top. The rite of passage to these riches is arduous. From administrative staff up through various loan officer and mid-level executive positions, the industry remains notorious for its meager wages.

❏ DECLINING SERVICE ON THE FRONT LINE

Banks are experiencing a dramatic change, as are many other industries in the United States, in the nature and composition of their work force. In short, banks are having difficulty identifying, recruiting, and retaining career-oriented, quality applicants for entry-level and intermediate-level positions. It is already evident to many industry observers and consumers that this is causing declining levels of service, while increasing the banks' costs of doing business.

Many tellers and administrative personnel have poor writing and verbal skills. Among foreign-born employees, mastery of basic English can be a problem. Frustration on the job, combined with exceedingly low wages, results in the early departure of many new hires.

Turnover among tellers, in fact, plagues the industry. Between resignations and terminations, many branch managers have their hands full simply trying to keep teller lines open. If it seems as if your bank has all new tellers every time you walk in, you may be right.

Bankers Monthly reported that the banking industry's biggest competitors for entry-level labor today are the dozens of fast-food franchisors who pay minimum wages. Banking and serving fast food are regarded as requiring similar sets of skills.

The national "teller problem" is not going to subside; many banks are already preparing to invest more heavily in advanced ATMs (Automated Teller Machines) and "tellerless" environments. The bank with the most advanced ATMs and/or most ATM locations may well be the bank of choice for many consumers in the near future.

☐ ANYONE CAN START A BANK

Another not widely known fact about the banking industry is that there are no professional barriers to starting a bank. More than a century ago, individuals such as J. P. Morgan; A. P. Giannini, founder of Bank of America; or H. Wells and G. W. Fargo were able to create institutions without any particular accreditation, licensing, or industry or government certification. This lack of professional requirements still exists in the banking industry.

Bankers enjoy lofty status in America, and a bank president in most communities is regarded as being on a par with the community's most prominent citizens, despite the fact that almost anyone can launch a new bank, almost as easily as he or she might launch any other kind of business. Furthermore, those who run banks are often shielded from the scrutiny of customers. Perhaps because they have control over so much money, we accord them the privileges that might be reserved for, say, a university president. While the S&L crisis has resulted in some change in the public perception of bankers, few of us ever inquire about a banker's credentials, academic record, educational achievements, or professional citations.

Though bankers are thought of as professionals, banking is one of the few professions that does not require standardized education or certification. There is no common body of knowledge with which bank counselors must be familiar before they can call themselves bankers, and no minimum standard of experience or competence that they must obtain to be accorded professional standing. There is certainly no established process of regular peer review.

However, many banking professionals today do have advanced degrees, such as masters of business administration (MBAs), although these, too, are not mandatory. Civil servants, undertakers, beauticians, barbers, and chiropractors all must pass more rigid examinations than your local banker.

While bankers can offer you sound financial guidance, the advice is no more reliable than the individual dispensing it and his or her willingness to serve your interests. It is important to recognize that bankers are men and women in business to make a profit. Only if the survival of their businesses is tied to the quality of service they provide will the level of customer service improve.

❑ SPOTTING A BANK IN TROUBLE

Normally, there is no need to investigate and follow your bank's financial health closely. It's difficult to get good information about a bank's financial status because banks can and do hide their problems, and the benefits of your research may be totally overshadowed by the time and costs involved. In addition, most consumers have far less than $100,000 in financial assets, so their deposits can be fully insured by Uncle Sam; even those with more than $100,000 can obtain full coverage if they divide their funds correctly among different accounts and banks. Only uninsured depositors or depositors who worry about the rare glitch that can keep them from gaining access to their funds when their bank fails should keep close tabs on their banks' financial health.

Those who need to keep tabs on their bank can spot telltale signs of trouble and chart their bank's current progress and development by taking the following measures:

□   Assess information closely.
□   Read bank correspondence.
□   Watch for key words that spell trouble.
□   Tap government and public resources.
□   Review bank reports and disclosure statements.
□   Speak frankly with bank officers.

Assess Information Closely

Most financial institutions work hard to maintain a conservative image of prudent management and financial health. From the enormous wooden desks and gray pinstripe suits to carefully worded advertisements, customer letters, and public relations campaigns, banks do everything they can to assure you that they are prospering, striving vehemently to keep bad news from leaking to the press.

When an embezzlement is discovered, for example, it is usually settled privately, rather than risking the bad publicity of a trial. The guilty party is merely terminated and must make a full payback. The point is, if you read about a bank that has made bad loans, has a celebrated customer or board member who is in financial difficulty, or is experiencing any other problem, the chances are excellent that the news is far worse than reported.

When it comes to bad news about banks, keep in mind, where there is smoke, there is probably a forest fire. In most cases, by the time you read an article about a bank that is encountering difficulties, the institution is either failing, about to close, or, at the least, severely threatened. When dealing with banks today, being cautious is a suitable approach to an industry whose health may be essential to yours.

Read Bank Correspondence

With the onslaught of direct-mail marketing, many people open their mail over the trash can. But correspondence from your bank concerns *your money*. Some banks insert valuable information into your monthly statement envelope alongside their innocuous advertisements for services they are trying to sell you. Though it is time-consuming, try to *read* all the correspondence you get from your bank.

If you don't understand the communication, call the bank and ask an officer to explain it. Banks today craft major announcements carefully, in some cases deliberately obscuring the meaning of what is happening, whether it be insolvency, lawsuits, or hostile takeovers.

Watch for Key Words That Spell Trouble

"Restructuring" historically has been used to mean that an institution is restructuring its assets. Today it can mean that a bank is scrambling to sell whatever it can, as quickly as it can, in an attempt to stay afloat.

Similarly, news of "management restructuring" or "realignment" often indicates demotions and/or mass firings resulting from performance disasters. An "earnings downturn" can mean anything from lower profits than in the previous reporting period to bankruptcy-threatening losses. Other terms that can indicate problems include: flat earnings, onetime losses, loan loss provision, nonperforming assets, conservatorship, assistance transaction, forbearance, and consent agreement.

Tap Government and Public Resources

Several government agencies, consumer organizations, and private firms can provide information to help you stay advised of your bank's strength and long-term viability. The National Technical Information Service (NTIS) can be of service. Federally insured financial institutions must provide quarterly "call reports" to their regulators. They are difficult reading, but if you are familiar with corporate financial terms and calculations, you will find these low-cost reports to be highly informative. Write to: NTIS, 5285 Port Royal Road, Springfield, VA 22161, or call 703-487-4000.

Your local public library, particularly if it has on-line services, can be an invaluable source of financial information. Using various indices, you can check for articles about bank officers and parent companies. If your bank has been in the news, the reference librarian can help you gather the information. A university library will be especially well stocked with information tools to help you in your investigation.

Review Bank Reports and Disclosure Statements

All federally insured institutions are required by law to provide an annual report at no charge to anyone who inquires. Therefore, commercial banks and savings-and-loan institutions make an annual disclosure statement, which you can request at any main office. Regardless of where you do your banking or where you choose to deposit your money, it is appropriate and prudent to ask the institution's investment department for its performance record.

Annual reports, 10Ks, and other disclosure statements are good resources for identifying banking officers and directors and for learning of the bank's expansion plans as well as the addresses and phone numbers of various divisions. These reports, along with interim quarterly reports, can be used as base information for a financial analysis of the bank. Because banks must also prepare comprehensive quarterly reports, the data you receive should never be too dated.

If the bank's volume of international loans is increasing, for example, this could indicate that the bank has left itself vulnerable to the risk of delayed paybacks in an attempt to achieve higher earnings. If the bank's equity or net worth is small relative to assets, or has been declining over time, the bank may not have the resources to continue meeting its obligations in the event of negative developments. If the bank has entered an expansion phase, this too may indicate a period of increased risk. In this case, make sure the bank has a long, strong, stable growth pattern, one that won't be seriously damaged by disappointing results during the expansion phase.

Keep in mind that all corporations have some leeway in how they compose their annual reports. The financial data as well as the accompanying descriptive passages they present may be designed to somewhat obscure their shortcomings. Disclosure statements must address certain issues in clear language, however, and they must provide potential investors with reliable information on which to base investment decisions. This is not to say that you should read only disclosure reports; a better strategy is to get all the data on your bank that you can.

In addition, the chief executive officer's report may disclose useful information, such as warnings in regard to "streamlining" operations (which may indicate the closing of some facilities), new products and services, and the diversification of current operations and services.

Consolidated income statements track the net revenue and percentage change over time and highlight any observed increases or decreases in bank revenues.

The auditor's letter indicates key bookkeeping changes, as well as any exceptions or notes to the financial statements. "Onetime" accounting entries and periodic changes in accounting methods may also be reported.

The Securities and Exchange Commission (SEC), based in Washington, requires your bank to file a 10K report on an annual basis. This document expands on the information contained in the annual report and includes additional documentation and "hard numbers." Although 10Ks are not readily distributed, your bank's report may be requested from the SEC for a fee, or from the institution itself at no cost. But you have to ask and go through proper channels.

Purchasing one share of stock is a relatively inexpensive and effective method of obtaining annual reports, 10Ks, quarterly reports, and entrance to shareholders' meetings.

Business periodicals offer special guides, special reports, and annual issues that cite performance records of financial institutions. Also, government agencies and regulatory bodies can provide a wealth of information on your bank and its history.

Speak Frankly with Bank Officers

Secrecy may be the goal of some bank officers, but that needn't stop you from speaking to them about any concerns you may have regarding your bank. If you believe that your bank is in trouble, consult with the branch manager or other key banker. A frank discussion with him or her regarding the bank's security may help you determine if there is any truth to your suspicions.

Ask about such matters as the bank's equity, whether it's operating at a profit, what type of growth is projected, and what percentage of problem loans it has on the books. Also ask if there have been any management turnover lately, revision of long-standing policies, or plans to restructure.

If the banker uses terms you do not understand, declines to acknowledge publicized losses, or otherwise dodges your questions, you may want to move your money to another bank.

How to Keep Your Money Safe

There is one silver lining to the savings-and-loan debacle. It soundly confirmed that the federal government will fulfill its promise to stand behind federally insured deposits in banks, credit unions, and savings-and-loans—even at a $500 billion price tag.

Deposits may be insured by the federal government under various providers, including the Federal Deposit Insurance Corporation's (FDIC's) Bank Insurance Fund (BIF), which covers bank deposits; the FDIC's Savings Association Insurance Fund (SAIF), which covers savings-and-loan deposits; and the National Credit Union Administration's (NCUA's) Share Insurance Fund, which covers credit union deposits. The protections are paid for in part by the individual institutions, but also through your tax dollars.

You can find out if a bank, credit union, or savings-and-loan is federally insured by reading the institution's literature, which will cite its insurance affiliation, for example, as "member FDIC." If you are uncertain, ask or look for the FDIC decal usually displayed on the windows or doors.

Be wary if an institution is covered by a state-regulated insurance fund, especially if that is the only coverage. In the last few years some state insurance funds did not have sufficient cash to cover their bank failures and some states chose not to make good on the obligations of their insurance agencies.

If you deposit less than $100,000 in a federally insured institution, all of your money will be federally insured. If you deposit more than $100,000, it still may be fully insurable if you follow the technical insurance coverage rules. Individuals with $200,000 in savings, for instance, can place $100,000 in a CD and the second $100,000 in an IRA. Because the second account is an IRA, both accounts can be established in the same individual's name and both accounts will be fully insured.

The technical coverage rules for deposits in excess of $100,000 can be complex. Because you must follow them to the letter to obtain full coverage, you should consult an investment adviser, attorney, or other qualified person. The FDIC in Washington, D. C., has staff specially trained to help consumers, free of charge, to understand the rules and how they apply in specific circumstances. You can call 800-424-5488 to reach these experts.

When a federally insured bank fails, it is usually purchased by another bank, which is normally much cheaper for the federal deposit insurance agency than liquidating the bank and paying off insured depositors.

There is no need to panic if your bank is taken over by another one. In most cases, this procedure runs very smoothly with no disruption of routine banking services or account accessibility. After the failed bank closes shop for the weekend, federal regulators and personnel from the acquiring bank peruse the records of the failed bank so it is ready to reopen, under a new name, on Monday.

You should be alerted to one problem, however. Your new bank may lower the high interest rate you were originally promised on your CD. This sometimes happens when the failed bank, in a final effort to stay afloat, attracted CD account holders by offering very high interest rates. When the insolvent bank is taken over, the acquiring bank may exercise its right to decrease the rates to market levels. This may seem unfair, but it happens. On the bright side, if you decide to move your funds elsewhere, you can close your CD account without an early withdrawal penalty.

If your federally insured bank fails and is not taken over by another bank, the federal government will move in. To get your money, you'll be asked to fill out an insurance claim form and have it notarized. This rarely occurs, but if it does, the procedure may take a few days or a few weeks. If your bank is out-of-state or further problems are encountered during the process, obtaining your money could take many weeks.

If your claim is contested because your bank left inaccurate or incomplete records on your acount, or worse, no records at all, you could be waiting for your money for months, though eventually it will come, provided you have your own proof of your deposits. To be safe, keep a small account at another bank for emergencies.

Once the government accurately identifies your proper balance, it makes arrangements for you to have access to your money by transferring it to another institution or issuing a check.

❏   **PRIVATE BANKING SERVICES**

During the 1970s, bankers discovered that the nouveau riche, or rising professional and managerial classes, represented a new business opportunity. Consequently, they began to develop more extensive "private" banking services to meet the needs of the most affluent 20 percent of their customers who now undertake the highest-value transactions and typically generate most of the bank's revenues. If you consider yourself to be among this group, you may qualify for these services at your local bank.

At the private banking hall of one of New York's biggest banks, at least two officers well acquainted with your finances will be available to meet your requests. You can obtain medium to high six-figure mortgage loans, often with no more difficulty than that of an average customer using an automatic teller machine.

The same bank will routinely arrange meetings to discuss your stock market transactions, long-term investment programs, and line-of-credit arrangements, among a host of other financial topics. Meanwhile, a rival bank across town will offer exclusive lectures on investment subjects such as precious metals, fine wines, and even Oriental rugs.

Another large New York bank offers customers with annual incomes of at least $300,000, or assets totaling $1 million, speedy turnarounds on loan applications, lower rates on larger lines of credit, and personalized investment advice. The bank will also provide a full range of financial services to its special customers, including restructuring estates, reviewing wills, and inventorying personal assets and liabilities. The bank's aim is to create a strategy for meeting the short- and long-term financial goals of its most successful clients, and to generate more business by awarding them special privileges.

For instance, a Florida bank will warehouse the furs, precious metals, paintings, and family heirlooms of its private banking customers. Six-figure depositors with a Texas bank have been allowed to borrow the bank's airplane, so long as they refill the tank when they're finished. A California bank will indulge some of its customers coast to coast by arranging private, high-powered networking with high-roller customers residing on the East Coast. For art lovers, the bank can provide appraisers from exclusive auctioneers as well as invitations to attend private collection previews before scheduled auctions.

A Colorado bank will offer "life cycle" financial services to those who qualify that include trust loans, deposit services, and investment management and counseling. A bank in Atlanta will provide free interest-bearing checking, preferred loan rates, CD bonuses, no annual fee on Gold MasterCard or Visa Gold, no-fee American Express Travelers Cheques, an exclusive ATM and ATM card, a free banking card, and other free services to its clients who meet certain income and account minimums.

Private banking services may be more in your range than you think. The American Bankers Association in Washington indicates that the vast majority of its members now have some type of plan to attract the newly affluent customer. The threshold beyond which you are accepted among the favored, however, varies within cities and regions, and bank to bank.

In some circles, a customer must be earning $100,000 per year and have half a million dollars in personal assets—excluding his or her residence or vacation home—to qualify for private banking services. At another bank, a checking-account balance of $12,000 and a savings account above $30,000 puts the customer in an exclusive category where all service fees are waived.

A well-established, suburban Philadelphia bank will assist certain customers with estate planning, setting up accounts, and providing custodial services, regular reports, and tax summaries in connection with their accounts. They will also make available a variety of life-insurance programs, line-of-credit programs, and retirement plans, and set up living and testamentary trusts.

Further, the bank will serve as a register and transfer or exchange agent for corporate security transactions, as well as trust depository, buying, selling, receiving, and delivering securities.

One St. Louis–area bank offers asset management services, financial planning, travel seminars, and other by-invitation-only perquisites to customers. It also provides "law office"–type services where special customers make deposits, buy CDs, sign paperwork for loans, and more. To qualify, customers place copies of their current tax return and financial statement on file at the bank.

A Washington state bank offers more than 10,000 of its well-to-do customers free checks, free checking, free safety deposit boxes, no-fee credit, and 24-hour access to a personal banker. To keep pace, four competitor banks have initiated similar services.

As the competition heats up, even customers in the $45,000 to $60,000 annual income range who are seen as potentially long-term customers—described as "homeowners with children"—become desirable and may be offered a variety of private banking services. The key to obtaining these valuable additional services is often little more than knowing enough to inquire about them.

It starts with a handshake   Private banking services are initially established face-to-face. Thereafter mail, phone, wire, and facsimile serve the special customer, often at the expense of service to other bank customers. Account managers keep special customers informed of new products, services, and rate variations. Some even actively relay data personally, if they know a particular customer would be interested in receiving it.

To find a bank in your area that offers private banking services, go shopping. In any metropolitan area of at least 200,000 people you can comparison-shop over the phone. In a matter of minutes you will know if you have reached a responsive, consumer-oriented institution interested in meeting your needs. Banks that have developed comprehensive, private banking services for customers with high-income or asset levels are only too happy to let inquirers know about them.

2

How to Decide
Where to Open an Account

Y OU DO NOT NEED TO USE ONE BANK FOR ALL YOUR BANKING
needs. You may want to open a checking account at one
bank, buy a CD at another, and take out a mortgage loan at a
third. Remember, we are using the term *bank* in its generic sense.
Banking services and products are available at commercial banks,
savings-and-loans, and credit unions. Investment products that
are very similar to some bank deposit accounts are also available
through stock brokerages and mutual funds.

If you want to be able to write checks against an account to pay
bills, you need some form of transaction, or checking, account.
Since deregulation, banks offer a confusing variety of transaction
accounts:

> *Regular checking:* Banks pay no interest on these accounts
> and frequently charge regular maintenance fees.
>
> *NOW (Negotiable Order of Withdrawal):* This account
> pays interest, usually at a modest rate, if the balance

exceeds a set minimum. It also requires monthly fees if the balance falls below that set minimum.

Super NOW: Banks often claim that this account pays "market rate" interest, but it does not always pay a higher interest rate than a NOW account. Balance requirements (both to avoid fees and earn interest) tend to be higher than with a NOW account.

☐   **COMMERCIAL BANKS**

Commercial banks offer a wide range of services, including checking accounts, savings accounts, trust facilities, and various types of loans. A commercial bank is chartered, either by a state government or by the federal government, to operate within a particular state. If state chartered, it will be controlled and regulated by the state banking commission. If federally chartered, it will be controlled and regulated by the Comptroller of the Currency. In all, there are more than 15,000 commercial banks in the United States, holding more than $2.5 trillion in assets.

Among dozens of possible criteria for choosing a bank, the following seem the most basic when deciding where to open a checking account:

- Find a bank that pays the highest net yields or imposes the lowest net costs.
- Choose a bank that is located near where you live, work, shop, or travel, and whose hours are convenient for you.
- Determine if the bank is a member of the FDIC's Bank Insurance Fund (BIF) for banks or Savings Association Insurance Fund (SAIF) for savings-and-loans or the NCU's Share Insurance Fund for credit unions.
- Select a bank where you can develop a relationship with a teller and branch manager, and where the quality of service is sufficiently high.

□ Choose a bank that has its own automated teller machines (ATMs) or belongs to an ATM network so that you can gain access to your cash quickly or when the bank is closed.

You should always look for an account that is federally insured and one that offers you the best return on your money. The importance you attach to the other factors will vary according to your banking preferences and habits. For example, if you know from past experience that you need frequent contact with bank personnel, you may be indifferent to whether a bank is a member of an ATM network. What you may find indispensable is living or working close to a bank's retail office.

On the other hand, you may be happiest when you can minimize visits to your bank. You may have your paycheck deposited directly into your account and use ATMs at the grocery stores and shopping malls to get your money. You may not care if you live or work near a bank so long as it is possible to get to the bank without killing yourself for infrequent visits. For you, what may be indispensable is access to a wide ATM network.

It may surprise you to know that some banks do not want your business. Some banks charge excessive service fees to *discourage* small accounts and charge depositors when the account holders seek to withdraw some of their funds. Among these banks, the prevailing strategy is to improve profitability by squeezing out smaller customers. If your bank seems to be discouraging your patronage, accommodate it and yourself by taking your business elsewhere.

If you determine that another institution would suit you better or charge you less for the services you require, don't be reluctant to switch. By some estimates, at least half of all banking consumers today could meet their banking needs better by either changing banks or switching accounts.

Relationship banking or "bundled accounts" may be the trend in the nineties, but having all your accounts at one institution does not necessarily mean you are being better served. It may save you service fees but result in lost earnings from interest-bearing accounts or higher credit card fees and annual charges.

☐ SAVINGS-AND-LOAN INSTITUTIONS

Traditionally, savings-and-loan institutions (S&Ls) were in business to provide savings plans and mortgage loans. Deregulation allowed S&Ls to expand their range of services, but today, over 75 percent of all loans issued by them are still mortgages.

Before deregulation, S&Ls relied on short-term savings deposits to fund long-term mortgages, which placed them in the most precarious position of all financial institutions. "Locked in" interest rates caused them to lose money on their loan portfolios when deposit interest rates skyrocketed in the 1970s and 1980s. These losses resulted in the failure of many savings-and-loans.

Following the failure of the FSLIC (Federal Savings and Loan Insurance Corporation), federally insured S&Ls were insured by the FDIC's Savings Association Insurance Fund (SAIF), which is in operation today. All told, there are more than 3,000 S&Ls across the United States.

Today, S&Ls provide most of the traditional banking services offered by commercial banks, including savings accounts, interest-bearing checking accounts (NOW accounts) and CDs. They also provide credit cards, home equity loans, and personal installment loans.

☐ CREDIT UNIONS

Credit unions are cooperative, nonprofit organizations formed to provide basic financial services for member depositors. Created by and for members of associations, unions, or employees of large institutions, more than 15,000 credit unions currently operate across the United States. Since deregulation, they can offer many services similar to those of commercial banks. For example, in addition to savings-type accounts, they offer share draft accounts that function like a checking account. They also offer personal loans, automobile loans, home equity loans, and mortgage loans.

Credit unions differ from the other institutions in a few major areas, all of which can translate into advantages for you.

1. Credit unions have no stockholders. These cooperatives neither pay dividends to stockholders nor do they pay federal income tax. These two areas of savings often enable credit unions to pay better rates to their depositors and charge lower rates to their borrowers.

2. Credit unions are prohibited by law from providing business loans. As a result, credit unions use their resources solely for developing and improving consumer services.

3. Federal credit unions are insured by what has been in recent years the strongest of the three federal deposit insurance programs.

☐   **NONTRADITIONAL SOURCES**

Should you have a significant sum to invest, say $10,000 or more, national brokerage houses and investment firms offer various asset-management or money-management accounts that may give you a higher return on your investment, with a correspondingly higher risk, than a commercial bank, credit union, or savings-and-loan institution. Many of these allow for unlimited check-writing privileges while your balance earns interest at competitive rates. Some allow only a fixed number of checks to be written each month. Many also levy a penalty if your account balance dips below a certain minimum. Terms vary widely, so find out what they are before you commit any money.

One prominent firm provides a free brokerage account with checking for an initial deposit of $5,000. The account comes with a free Visa debit card, pays daily interest, and offers 24-hour service and commission discounts. Most of these services include toll-free telephone numbers. However, most accounts at brokerage houses are not insured. As stated previously, your money is safest in a federally insured account.

☐ THE STORY BEHIND BANK FEES

When you open your monthly bank statement, you may see a charge for $7, for example, to "maintain" your checking account. If your savings account dips below $100, it may cost you another $2. You may pay an annual fee of $20 or $25 for your credit card. A returned check can cost you $30. What is going on? Is this a consumer rip-off, or is this just the cost of doing business with a bank in the nineties?

Before deregulation, savings and checking accounts were free. Because of interest rate ceilings, a bank's interest costs were low in relation to its interest earnings. Consequently, banks could make an easy profit without relying on deposit fee income.

Since deregulation, banks have increased the interest rates they pay on some of their deposits. Generally speaking, the higher rates are paid on deposits with high balances. To offset this new cost, banks are imposing fees for deposit services that used to be free.

Consumers with little savings to keep on deposit are hardest hit by the way banks now price their services. Because service fees may totally offset any interest earnings, consumers in this category may not be able to find a bank that pays them net earnings. Their best bet may be to find the bank that charges the least.

On the other hand, consumers with $1,000 or more to keep in a checking account may obtain a net gain on their money from the new price structures. Look for the bank that pays the highest yield.

Service Fees Continue to Increase

Particularly in urban areas, bank fees have escalated enormously. Some institutions are charging $8 a year to "maintain" your Individual Retirement Account, $15 to stop a check, $4 for a cashier's check, and so on.

When you accidentally "bounce" a check, there can be a $30 service charge, depending on where you bank. Banks often justify such a fee by claiming they are merely recouping staff costs of handling your bounced check. A Federal Reserve Board report, however, indicated that the real cost of a returned check to a bank in the late eighties averaged only 36¢, which means that banks charging $30 may be making nearly 1,000 percent profit.

From 1984 to 1988, fees for NOW accounts rose by an average of 56 percent, but differed widely among banks. One survey of 73 banks and 69 S&Ls revealed that a hypothetical customer with $300 to $500 in a NOW account paying 5.25 percent interest would earn up to $11 or pay as much as $172 per year, depending on where he or she banked.

Only the Beginning of Rising Fees

Rising bank fees may long be with us. Analysts predict that the increasing range of bank services will be accompanied by ever-increasing service fees. However, because a growing portion of the population—nearly 16 million American families, or one out of every six—cannot afford checking accounts and finds it difficult to pay bills, obtain credit, or cash checks, consumer advocates and some members of Congress have proposed requiring banks and savings-and-loan associations to offer consumers a "basic" or "lifeline" no-frills account. A basic account could be opened with a minimum deposit of only $25, would have no minimum balance requirement, and would provide 10 checks a month. Banks could charge enough for the service to recoup all their costs and make a 10 percent profit.

❏ ## THE OVERWHELMING CASE
FOR SHOPPING AROUND

A librarian found that she had paid $168 in the past twelve months to maintain two interest-bearing checking accounts at a bank where she had her IRAs, savings account, Visa card, and home-equity loan. When she spoke with the branch manager, she was advised to wait a month for the bank's "new" product, which would allow her free checking with a $10,000 deposit in a savings account.

She considered the new product suggestion to be rather ridiculous; if she had $10,000 in her present accounts, she would not be paying any fees anyway.

Unwilling to comply with this unreasonable solution, she asked for a printed fee schedule from the bank. As it turned out, an interest-bearing checking account required a $1,500 average monthly balance to avoid monthly fees. However, she also discovered the following hidden costs:

Overdraft	$20.00
Return check fee	20.00
Stop payment	15.00
Certified check	8.00
Photostat (copy of item)	3.00
Wire transfer	10.00
Reconciling bank statement	10.00/hr
Non-bank ATM withdrawal	1.00
Non-bank ATM inquiry	0.75

Three dollars for a customer copy of bank records? The librarian was upset. At this point, fed up with being dollared and dimed to death, she began checking competitive banks in her neighborhood. A stable, large institution near her home offered a more competitive package. A $1,000 minimum balance in a regular checking account at this bank gave her free checking, free ATM services, and a free Visa card. She opened an account there the next day.

Figuring Out Which Checking Account Is the Best Deal

To identify your best deal in a checking account, consider both the interest an account will pay and the fees it requires you to pay. Since interest earnings and fees frequently vary according to your account balance and other factors, a "good deal" account for one consumer may be a "bad deal" account for another.

Analyze the terms of each account in light of your own financial circumstances and habits. For example, if your account balance usually falls below $500 during a month, an account paying a relatively high interest rate may be a bad deal if it also imposes a fee on balances that fall below $500. If you are confident that your account will always exceed the minimums required to avoid fees, make your final account selection on the basis of the interest you can earn.

Here again, account yields often vary according to your account's balance. For example, a bank may pay an attractive rate on accounts with balances above $1,000, but either nothing or a lower rate on accounts that fall below that minimum. If you can exceed the minimum, this account may be the best for you. If you can't, it may be a bad deal, particularly if you will be penalized by paying monthly fees.

Pay particular attention to the minimum balance rules. Banks usually base fee waivers on the lowest balance in the account during the month, or on the average daily balance during the month. Look for an account that determines fees on the average daily balance since that balance is always going to be higher than your lowest balance (unless your account balance does not fluctuate at all).

Similarly a bank may look to either the average daily balance or the lowest balance to determine whether to pay interest (or the rate of interest it wants to pay). Again, you are more likely to earn interest if the minimum balance rule is based on the average daily, not the lowest balance.

Finally, some banks have historically used unfair and deceptive balance calculation methods when paying interest. Assume that your account earns interest at an annual rate of 7 percent, or .583 percent monthly. Also assume that your average daily balance was $500 during the previous month, but on day 28, after paying your monthly bills, your account balance fell to $200.

Some banks will apply the .583 percent to the lowest balance, or $200, as if you only had $200 in your account throughout the month. Others, ones that use the "investable" balance method, apply the .583 percent rate to only a portion, usually 88 percent, of the average daily balance. You will get the best deal with accounts that pay on the *full* daily or average daily balance.

Soon you will not have to worry about banks calculating interest on less than your full balance. On the final day of the 1991 session, Congress passed the Truth-in-Savings Act. That law, long sought by consumer advocates, requires all banks to pay interest on the full amount in your account each day. It becomes effective in early 1993.

A final caveat: Do not be fooled by claims about frequent interest-rate compounding. Compounding means that the interest added to your account, left untouched, earns interest on itself. With monthly compounding, $\frac{1}{12}$ of your predicted annual interest is added. With daily compounding, $\frac{1}{365}$ of your predicted annual interest is added. Keeping $1,000 in your checking account at 6 percent, with monthly compounding, yields an interest payment of $5.00 for the first month, $5.025 for the second month (6 percent $\times$ $\frac{1}{12}$ $\times$ $1,005), $5.05 for the third month (6 percent $\times$ $\frac{1}{12}$ $\times$ $1,010.025) and so on.

The frequency of compounding only becomes significant over long periods of time and then only for larger balances. For example, assume you kept $1,500 on deposit for a year in each of two accounts earning 5.5 percent annual interest. The difference in earnings during the year between the account that compounds daily and the one that compounds quarterly is a meager 62 cents.

On the other hand, on a $10,000 deposit in a 5-year CD, compounding differences can make a big difference in earnings. At 8 percent compounded daily the $10,000 earns $4,917.58. At 8 percent compounded annually it earns $4693.28.

Other fees may make a difference for you. For example, if because of your particular circumstances, you anticipate frequent or even occasional stop payment, overdraft, returned check, or other special fees, figure them into your calculations when comparison shopping. If you cannot avoid overdraft fees by keeping a high balance in your account, you may still be able to avoid them by getting an overdraft line of credit. Some banks charge $30 or even $50 if they receive a check drawn against insufficient funds, even though the check is returned unpaid with no loss to the bank. At that rate, one or two overdrafts can totally wipe out a year's interest earnings on a modest balance.

Here are the basic questions to ask when trying to identify which account will pay you the highest net earnings (or charge you the lowest net costs).

Questions Related to Costs

◻ What is the minimum balance I have to keep in my account for free checking?

◻ How is that balance computed? Is it the lowest balance during the month? The average daily balance during the month? Or something more unusual?

◻ Do balances in my other accounts count toward the minimum balance for my checking? If no, why not?

◻ What are the fees if I slip below that minimum?

◻ Is there a cost per check if I slip below the minimum? How much is it?

◻ Can I get an ATM card? What are the charges? Is there a fee for the card itself?

◻ Is there a fee for using one of the bank's own ATMs? What is the fee if I use an ATM within the network but not owned by the bank?

◻ What are the fees for a returned check? A stop payment?

◻ Can I get an overdraft line of credit?

◻ How much does it cost to order printed checks?

Questions Related to Earnings

- □ What is the annual interest rate or rates?
- □ What minimum balance must I maintain in the account to get the rate or rates? Is this minimum requirement based on the lowest balance during the month or the average daily balance during the month?
- □ Is the interest rate paid on my average daily balance, or does the bank use unfair practices such as paying on the lowest balance or the investable balance?
- □ How often is interest compounded? Quarterly? Daily? Annually? (This question is only relevant for large balances, about $5,000 or greater.)

Consider Accounts Offered by S&Ls and Credit Unions

Currently, S&Ls may offer better checking account deals than commercial banks, but don't forget the possibility of arranging for this service through a credit union. About 75 percent of America's credit unions offer their version of checking called "share drafts." Most credit unions charge no regular service fees, though some require a minimum balance of a few hundred dollars to avoid service fees.

A possible drawback of credit unions is that many do not return checks to the account holder at the end of the month. Instead they photocopy your checks after they clear your account, store them for a period of time, and then destroy them. This is one reason why credit unions can offer checking accounts at a reasonable fee.

If you need a life-size copy of a check for proof of payment, you can always purchase it from the credit union, usually for a nominal fee. Ask what it would cost, however, before deciding if this system is right for you. Also, consider the hassle of not having your canceled checks readily at your disposal when someone claims you did not pay a bill, or when it comes time to compute your taxes.

In assessing which bank's checking account is the best for you, consider net earnings or costs by subtracting anticipated costs from anticipated earnings. For example, suppose you encounter an institution that pays only 4 percent interest but charges no monthly service fees. You may find that you're better off with this particular account than with one that pays 6 percent interest annually but charges $5 a month if you drop below a specified minimum balance.

Senior citizen and student discounts Many banks provide these two special groups a basic checking account (no interest) with no fees.

The "Asset Management" Account

With higher deposit account balances, you may want to look for a bank or other financial institution that offers an "asset management" account. If you will be maintaining accounts with more than $5,000, on which you want to write checks, a different set of conditions may become important.

Brokerage houses offer asset management accounts that require initial deposits of $5,000 to $25,000, with annual management fees ranging from $25 to $150. If you already have other investments in stocks and bonds that meet the minimum balance requirement, this may be an option for you.

❏ WHAT IS THE BEST ACCOUNT FOR SAVINGS

Although most consumers have money in a passbook or statement savings account, there may be better places to store your savings. First, let us review the nonchecking account options available through banks, S&Ls, and credit unions.

Savings accounts These accounts can be the easiest way to earn some interest on small amounts of money while keeping the money accessible. On the other hand, these accounts, which include passbook accounts and statement accounts, can eat away at your hard-earned savings if they require regular maintenance fees. With passbook accounts, the bank enters the transaction and current balance in a passbook each time you make a deposit or withdrawal. With statement accounts "in-person" transactions are not necessary. The bank sends you a monthly or quarterly statement documenting your account activity.

Money market accounts These are also called money-market deposit-accounts (MMDAs). Although they allow limited check writing, they are primarily a savings account. In general, only three checks can be written against the account each month. Banks claim to pay "market rates" on these accounts, but frequently they pay their best rates only on larger balances. Indeed, since banks also impose hefty fees if a minimum balance is not maintained, these accounts are often the worst deal for small savers.

Certificates of deposit (CDs) CDs are a simple way to earn higher yields than those available on savings accounts. Their main drawback, which may not be a drawback for some, is their time restrictions. You have to select the time period you are willing to leave your funds in the account when you open the CD. Common time period options are 30, 60, or 90 days, 1 year and 5 years.

Many banks, but not all, impose an early withdrawal penalty if you withdraw your funds before the preselected time period expires. Usually no other fees apply. The longer the term and the larger the deposit, the higher the interest rate the bank is usually willing to pay.

If you have $2,000 or less in savings and you need ready access to those funds, your best bet may be a statement or passbook savings account. Alternatively, you should consider combining your savings with the money you keep in your checking account. You may earn the highest yield by combining both accounts into one of the interest-paying checking or transaction accounts now available. This strategy may produce the balance you need to avoid both checking and savings account fees and earn the best interest rate.

Even statement and passbook savings accounts usually require minimum balances to avoid fees. These minimums are usually in the $100 to $500 range, although some banks set their minimums at $1,000 or more.

Most banks also have minimum balance requirements for earning interest on regular savings accounts. At some banks, these minimums are at the $1,000 or more level. Usually, however, these minimums are less than $100.

Just as they do with checking accounts, some banks play games when they calculate the interest a savings account has earned. Our advice here is the same as in our discussion on checking accounts: Find a bank that pays interest on the full daily, or average daily balance. You will not have to worry about this in early 1993, when the 1991 Truth-in-Savings Act takes effect. All banks will have to pay interest on your full balance by using one of these two balance methods.

A MMDA may be the worst place to deposit savings of $2,000 or less because of the high minimum balance often required. Many banks require you to keep more than $2,000 on deposit to earn interest. Balances that fall below the minimum may earn no interest at all. Similarly, unless high balances are maintained, significant fees (such as $10 per month) kick in.

If you have $500 or more to invest, and you have no need for ready access to the funds, consider a CD. In choosing the account term or duration, be careful not to overextend yourself. If you need to withdraw funds from the CD before the term expires, you could lose significant interest earnings.

Also consider a bank's renewal—or rollover—policies and terms. Some banks give consumers a 7- to 14-day grace period that begins when the original term expires. During the grace period, the consumer can withdraw his or her funds to switch banks or accounts without suffering an early withdrawal penalty. Without a grace period, you may find yourself locked into a bad renewal rate when your CD automatically rolls over at the end of its original term.

❑ BANK CREDIT CARDS

Another one of your high-priority items may be obtaining a major credit card such as Visa or MasterCard. Consumers have become very dependent on bank credit cards and for good reason—they offer enormous advantages if used wisely.

Credit cards allow you to keep simple records of business and entertainment expenses. They also enable you to take care of emergencies, such as car repairs on the road, shelter at a hotel in a snowstorm, replacing a broken appliance, or seeing a doctor. In addition, you can get a cash advance during a family crisis or take advantage of special advertised airline fares.

Using these cards can, of course, crush a budget and lead to financial ruin. Responsible use includes knowing the fees and interest charges associated with them. With credit cards, as with deposit accounts, comparison shopping is vital. Do not assume that the bank you choose for your deposits should be the bank you choose for a credit card.

There are three key questions to ask in shopping for your piece of plastic:

□ What is the annual fee?
□ What is the annual percentage rate (APR) charged? Is the interest rate variable? If so, what index is used to calculate the rate? How often can the rate change?
□ Is there a grace period during which no interest charges are incurred?

Keep in mind that if you *do not* pay the balance during the grace period, the interest rate is the major factor to consider in shopping for a credit card; if you *do*, the annual fee is the major factor.

Most banks offer you Visa or MasterCard accounts but the annual fees and interest they charge vary widely. In some cases, you will find there is no annual fee at all provided you maintain a large amount of cash in a savings account. In other cases, you will pay as much as $40 per year.

Interest charges can vary widely as well, from 12 percent to more than 21 percent per year. Some banks allow you a grace period during which no fee is charged, provided you have paid off the previous month's balance in full.

Cash Advance Fees

Some banks have steep "cash advance" fees in addition to the interest charge. At one bank, for example, a credit card cash advance of $1,000 would incur a $25 flat fee plus a 16.00 percent interest charge on the unpaid balance. Therefore, at the end of the month, your statement would indicate that you owe $26.75, which equals 32.1 percent interest per year.

Also, any payments that you have made to your account are first deducted from your balance for purchased goods and services, a balance that usually involves a lower interest rate. Your cash advance balance, with its higher interest rate, remains on your monthly statement until your entire balance on purchases is fully paid. At all times, the terms of any credit card are readily available to you from the sponsoring institution, though usually in very fine print. Recent changes in Regulation Z require credit card issuers to disclose the key terms of the card (the annual fee, APR, and grace period) in a simple-to-understand table. Lenders are required to give you this information in print at the time you receive an application. Before completing a credit card application, collect several applications, compare the federal disclosure boxes, and choose the card that costs you the least and provides the most benefits. Also, be aware that rates can and often do change between the time you complete an application and the time you start using your card.

Over-the-limit fees can be extremely high with some cards, adding a penalty as high as $20 per month. "Late" charges can cost as much as $240 a year. Conceivably, one could end up making a monthly payment that largely addresses penalties and only reduces the outstanding balance by a few dollars.

3

Who's Who at Your Bank

T O MAKE YOUR BANK WORK FOR YOU, IT IS USEFUL TO HAVE AN insider's perspective of the various staff positions. Depending on the size of your bank, the titles of manager, department head, and officer may be interchangeable. The larger the institution, the greater the level of specialized expertise among the job classifications. Consequently, when meeting a bank manager or staff member for the first time, it is a good idea to find out beforehand exactly what that person's responsibilities are and how long he or she has held the position.

According to the American Institute of Banking, only about 25 percent of the total number of people working in the financial services industry hold management positions. The remaining 75 percent fill "back office" positions, including tellers, support personnel in the consumer and commercial loan departments, accountants, marketing specialists, bank-card employees, mortgage loan officers, computer programmers and data processing operators, secretaries and administrative assistants, security guards, maintenance personnel, and so on. The bank may also have a cadre of "consultants" who perform special services on a retainer basis or by charging an hourly fee. Here are some of the staff you may meet, starting at the branch level:

> branch managers
> assistant branch managers
> head tellers
> tellers

☐   **BRANCH MANAGERS**

Branch managers often function with great autonomy. They are responsible for the day-to-day operation of the branch, including the supervision of staff, providing reports to the main office in accordance with established procedures, overseeing cash management, and directing all aspects of customer service. Some managers may supervise one function only, such as new accounts, commercial loans, or Individual Retirement Accounts (IRAs).

Usually, whatever can be done at the main office can be done at any of its branches. The branch can approve personal and commercial loans, offer a variety of investments, set up trust funds and club accounts, as well as issue traveler's checks and make cash advances on credit cards. A branch manager can also act as the proverbial "good samaritan" within his or her community by becoming involved in local civic affairs. In fact, such a role is usually encouraged by senior management in an effort to increase the bank's visibility and attract new customers.

Since the job of the branch manager is to generate business, establishing a personal relationship with him or her could be mutually beneficial. If you are planning to purchase a new car, ask the branch manager about financing options. Discuss your financial plans for your child's education. Find out about IRAs. A random survey of bankers around the country supports the view that developing a good working relationship with your banker is much more important than you might think.

☐ ASSISTANT BRANCH MANAGERS

An assistant branch manager handles most of the same tasks as a branch manager except liaison with the main office, weekly and monthly reporting, and perhaps marketing.

☐ HEAD TELLERS

Some large banks and branches may have an official or unofficial head teller who supervises the other tellers, but who otherwise performs all the other functions of a regular teller. The head teller may have the power to approve some transactions in the absence of a branch manager or relieve a branch manager's assistant of some routine responsibilities.

☐ TELLERS

The basic function of accepting deposits and making withdrawals has changed as the needs of customers have become more complicated and diverse. Tellers, or "customer service representatives," are trained to handle all of your daily routine transactions, such as selling you traveler's checks, money orders, certified or cashier's checks, and cashing your personal checks. He or she will also accept your loan payments and may even give you loan advances or make withdrawals against your established line of credit.

The bank teller is your first line of communication regarding bank services. The teller is also your first source for the resolution of account problems. With a computer terminal in front of each teller, many of your questions can be answered by any one of them with on-the-spot account research.

As a rule, tellers are poorly paid. Even top-earning tellers earn less than many office secretaries. The higher salaries are paid to full-time workers with experience and a significant length of service with the bank. Turnover in the industry is high.

Tellers are closely supervised. Since they come into contact with more customers daily than any other employee, some banks rely on them for cross-selling bank services and products. They must be familiar with all types of accounts and know how to serve customers in a number of areas. As employees of the bank, tellers are subject to the bank's policies and procedures, as well as federal, state, and local banking regulations and guidelines.

Especially in a large urban location, tellers may serve customers at the rate of at least one every five minutes. This means that a typical teller deals with more than 100 customers every day.

A Good Relationship with a Bank Teller Is Vital

Try to develop a first-name relationship with a head teller. If possible, work with that person exclusively. If you stop to consider a teller's typical day, you will quickly see why, after only a few pleasant encounters, he or she will manage your accounts with extra care and attention.

A good relationship with a teller can save you a great deal of inconvenience. If you leave your cashier's checks on the counter or discover a deposit error, a shortfall in a cash withdrawal, or other irregularity, it is simpler to call the bank and ask for a specific individual by name. By the same logic, if you find an error on your bank statement, or discover that a transaction by mail was mishandled, a working relationship with a teller can lead to a rapid correction of the mistake.

❏   **BANK MANAGEMENT**

Board of Directors

The bank's board of directors is a group of appointed or elected senior officials, both from within the bank and from the community at large, that meets periodically throughout the year and sets the bank's general policies. Board membership is usually composed of the bank's chief executive officer and president, several of the bank's vice-presidents, such as the comptroller and director of operations, and prominent shareholders not employed by the bank. Outside members, not necessarily banking experts, are selected based upon success in their own fields of endeavor. There is a strong element of prestige associated with being a board member, particularly of a large bank. Directors are able to exchange business ideas with one another, and membership tends to enhance their visibility.

Often, those who get appointed or elected to a board are well connected to officers of the bank. Board members for national and international banks include some of the top executives and leaders in the world. Former U.S. presidents, cabinet members, ambassadors, and statesmen are often asked to serve on boards, and often do.

There are several publications available in public libraries that provide information about directors. Standard and Poor's *Register of Directors and Executives* gives the names, telephone numbers, and business and home addresses of 75,000 executives with biographies-in-brief that list their directorships, other business affiliations, and alma maters, as well as approximate annual revenues of the directors' own companies. Directors from outside the bank are paid for their services in excess of $150 per hour.

A board may convene nine or ten times a year, depending on circumstances. Board members have an important role to play in ensuring the health and viability of the bank. They advise the executive staff on responsibilities to shareholders, customers, and employees. Members of the board know who's who in the community, which projects are going forward, who is failing, and who is making money.

Their job is basically to gather information that bears on the overall profitability of the bank. They create policies and determine the direction of the bank's business, expansions, and capital improvements.

Chief Executive Officer

Organizational structure varies from bank to bank, but most have a chief executive officer (CEO) or president who directs the bank's operations. The CEO is usually in charge of working with other senior managers and executives in the bank's business community, as well as with supervising the performance of other bank officers.

Often a bank's CEO can be found on the boards of the community's most prestigious civic, social, and charitable associations. In fact, a bank's CEO is sometimes the president or vice-president of such boards. In major metropolitan areas, the CEOs of large banks are frequently found on the boards of major corporations and institutions.

Vice-Presidents

Banks will usually have several vice-presidents who supervise specific bank departments. A comptroller or cashier is usually an executive officer in charge of the bank's physical property. Another executive officer may be in charge of operations with the title, chief operations officer (COO). A treasurer or chief financial officer (CFO) manages the money required to operate the bank.

Other executive officers may be charged with corporate marketing, information systems (chief information officer), human resources, and other components of the organization.

Senior management people institute policy decided by the bank's board of directors, and try to operate the institution for a profit. They may handle budgeting, maintain responsibility for bringing in large accounts, monitor long-term staffing needs, and evaluate corporate and branch performance.

In recent years, job title inflation has crept into the banking business. Several people may carry the title of vice-president, marketing, for example, presumably to give them an edge as they attempt to generate business for the bank.

Bank VPs, managers, and officers also often serve on boards of one or more civic or philanthropic associations. In addition, community contacts, experience in other institutions, and success in other fields are pluses for upwardly mobile banking managers.

Loan Officers

Loan officers in small banks may be empowered to offer all manner of loans to consumers and businesses. In large institutions, these functions may be specialized. One loan officer may provide personal or installment loans; another may approve commercial, real estate, and agricultural loans; yet another may be in charge of second mortgages and home equity loans.

Business loan officers usually have backgrounds in finance, commercial law, federal and state regulations, or economics. They generally have a sound knowledge of overall business practices.

Making high-volume, profitable loans is one of the bank's chief income vehicles, by which loan officers advance their careers. If you run a business, they can also provide services such as payroll management, financial systems, or pension management.

Business loan officers are eager to develop long-term client relationships. The more familiar your business is to loan officers, the smaller their perceived risk in giving you a loan. In fact, many of them appreciate meeting potential customers who do not need money right away.

Financial Service Officers

A financial service officer or financial planner works basically in a sales capacity, often relying heavily on the commission income earned through the sale of investment products. Look for individuals with solid experience, who have your needs in mind—not just what the bank has to offer. A good financial service officer can also help you set up an investment portfolio.

Bank officers in trust management work with families to set up estates that meet their personal and financial goals. They should know state and federal tax laws and have extensive knowledge about stocks, bonds, mutual funds, and other investment options.

Bank Examiners

As part of the bank regulatory system, and therefore important to the bank management organization, the bank examiner profoundly influences operations. Bank examiners are *not* employed by the banks; they are employed by the Federal Deposit Insurance Corporation and other federal or state agencies. The savings-and-loan crisis notwithstanding, bank examiners are responsible for preventing bank failures. Their job is to investigate unsafe and unfair banking practices and violations of federal regulations.

During a safety and soundness examination, a bank examiner assesses the organization of the bank and its financial health, including the bank's outstanding loans. These findings are presented to the bank's senior management with recommendations for improvement. Bank examiners are experienced in accounting and auditing procedures as well as analyzing investments and loan processing.

During a consumer examination, an examiner looks through loan files, sales literature, and training manuals to determine whether the bank is complying with the Truth-in-Lending Act, the Community Reinvestment Act, and other consumer protection laws.

❏ GAIN GREATER LEVERAGE AT YOUR BANK

The following ideas, if properly executed, will help you gain greater leverage when dealing with bank personnel:

Don't Be Intimidated

Under the current system, banks can be intimidating places in which to discuss your personal finances. Yet, banks simply could not exist without customers. Keep in mind that it is your money that enables them to stay in business.

Negotiate for What You Want

Negotiate for the services and benefits you value. Ask for no-fee credit cards, overdraft protection, more favorable interest rates and terms for certificates of deposit, money markets funds, and NOW accounts. Seek free safe-deposit boxes, free checking, and low-interest loans.

Own a Piece of the Bank—Buy Stock

Companies, including banks, sell stock for one reason—to raise money. If they want to expand, invest in new equipment, develop a new product or service, or buy out the competition, they can either borrow money from private sources or sell stock.

A share of your bank's stock probably sells for $100 or less. By owning stock, you won't necessarily receive equal monetary compensation in the form of services; rather, it gives you the power to vote. You may be able to leverage that power into better service, and you can take your complaints to the top through annual shareholders' meetings.

A company like other companies Your bank is a legal corporation in its own right regulated by local, state, and federal law. A corporation is owned by stockholders but run by a board of directors and bank employees. The stockholders elect the board of directors. The board of directors select the bank's officers including the chief executive officer, the president, and other bank "trustees" who oversee the day-to-day operations of the bank (including the services you receive as a customer).

The stockholders and the board of directors determine the direction and policy that is executed by the bank employees. The bank's annual report and quarterly financial report will list the number of shares of stock outstanding, the average trading price for that quarter, and the exchange on which it is traded.

Check the financial section of your local paper for the recent trading price. If your bank offers discount brokerage services, then buy the bank's stock through the bank.

Share Your Plans

Discuss your investment plans with your banker. Mention that a secure return on your investment is important to you. See what ideas the banker has for investing your money and at what rate. Ask about estate planning or setting up a trust fund for your child.

4

Conducting Your
Transactions Quickly

T IME IS AN INCREASINGLY VALUABLE COMMODITY. DUAL-INCOME couples and single parents are the rule rather than the exception. There is little opportunity during the day for employed individuals to take care of errands. For this reason, department stores stay open until late in the evening and on weekends, the cleaners usually do not close before 7:00 P.M., and many supermarkets are open 24 hours a day. But many banks continue to keep banker's hours.

WHY BANKING HOURS
REMAIN INCONVENIENT

Banker's hours were established in the past century to provide clerks the hours of daylight to post all the transactions in the bank's ledgers by hand. Today banks explain their hours by claiming that their computer operators need time to post all their transactions electronically. They observe that since the individual consumer maintains a greater number of accounts than in the past (savings, checking, IRAs, NOW, etc.), bookkeeping is more complex, even though people are no longer writing numbers on ledger books by gaslight.

Some time *is* required for information transfer because of the problems associated with bank automation. The equipment that sorts and moves checks from some financial institutions is located in another city. Check posting for one of the world's largest credit unions, for example, is accomplished from a suburban office building hundreds of miles from its branch offices.

Many older and more established banks were automated in a piecemeal fashion. Hardware and software were purchased to perform one function or another instead of achieving the goal of managing the bank's total information. As a result, bank managers were saddled with expensive, but nonintegrated, equipment. One machine may be required to gain access to your checking account, another to your IRA.

Off-Line, Out of Touch

For smaller institutions, the mainframe and software that maintain bank records are likely to be owned and operated by an independent company in another location. Bank branches may not be on-line or "live" with the main office. Even in this electronic age, many banks still send tapes of batch transactions to an outside business every afternoon to be downloaded into the main office's information system. If you have seen your teller dial a phone to get your account balance or last check number processed, he or she is not on-line with the bank's computer.

So, while the electronic data-processing industry has kept pace with the component products and services that banks have added, these technological advances have not had much impact on banking hours. Although competition has forced some banks to open one evening a week or Saturday morning, for the most part, banking remains inconvenient. Finding time during the business day to get your banking done is a challenge; when you do, the lines are often long and the service is slow. The typical bank schedule is 9:00 A.M. to 3:00 P.M., Monday through Friday.

The most popular and convenient alternatives to waiting in line are the following:

□ Electronic funds transfer, such as automated teller machines (ATMs), direct deposit, automatic loan payment programs, and preauthorized payment of recurring bills
□ Bank-by-mail
□ Bank-by-phone
□ Bank-by-personal-computer
□ Wire transfers

□   **THE ELECTRONIC FUNDS TRANSFER**

Computer technology has made it possible to transfer money instantly, and many banks today give customers immediate access to their accounts through a variety of automated services. The electronic funds transfer (EFT) system is meant to be an asset to the bank by cutting its processing costs and adding a convenience for its customers. Sometimes, though, automation works to the consumer's disadvantage. Errors can be difficult to prove and can be expensive.

The Cost of "Mismanaged" Electronic Transfers

Unless electronic services are managed properly, automated systems may extract excessive service charges from your account, damage your credit rating, and wreak havoc with your cash flow and interest. Conducting your banking electronically requires that you protect yourself by maintaining all records of your transactions.

☐ ## THE AUTOMATED TELLER MACHINE,
A 24·HOUR·A·DAY TELLER

This twentieth-century wizard machine got off to a slow start in the early seventies. One bank president recalled that a couple of years ago his bank's machines were disaster areas. They incurred major foul-ups on deposits that cost the bank dearly. Initially, the high rate of error and the debugging of the ATMs were as expensive for the banks as the machines themselves. Consider the capital investment to set up ATM systems: The initial cost of one ATM exceeds $25,000, with another $10,000 or so for software and installation. When you add the costs of the service contract, routine maintenance, security systems, and telephones, the investment soon becomes staggering.

About 25 percent of ATM-equipped banks have defrayed these expenses in part by charging consumers to use them. At some banks, you will incur up to a $1 charge for a cash withdrawal of any size. If you are a frequent ATM user, it pays either to find a bank with no ATM charges, or to make larger, less frequent transactions.

Today, most of the bugs are out of the system, the machines work, and banks have found new uses for them. For example, many banks now participate in regional or national ATM networks. In fact, of the approximately 60,000 ATMs in the United States, more than a third are members of ATM networks, such as Plus or Cirrus, which enable you to withdraw your cash, pay your bills, or check your balance from an out-of-state location. These networks now include more than 700 banks and S&Ls.

Nevertheless, even though the reliability of ATMs has improved, 60 percent of banking consumers do not use them, preferring face-to-face transactions. Some people fear, perhaps rightly, that around-the-clock availability of their money will lead them into overspending. Others fear being robbed, dislike carrying another card, or think ATMs are prone to errors.

Bankers are enthusiastic about the future of ATMs, however,

and many look forward to putting them to use in ways that do not seem plausible now. New machines are being designed to give exact change, including coins, and provide more services to further reduce your time inside the bank. In addition, some institutions are considering ATMs that dispense postage stamps and take loan applications from you. You may also be able to buy stocks, mutual funds, and insurance policies through ATMs in the future.

Utilizing the ATM

The ATM is useful for far more than getting cash on a Sunday afternoon; it is often accessible 24 hours a day, 7 days a week. Enabling you to avoid going to the bank for most of your business, this machine will display your balance, take deposits, transfer funds, allow you to pay certain credit card bills, and provide receipts for all these transactions.

Most automated teller machines will accept deposits for more than one account at the same institution. Your bank may assign you a second access code to designate the second account. When you make a *deposit* with the ATM, you select the account and code you want. An envelope is provided for your use.

Your ATM deposit receipt is a provisional receipt, to be confirmed by the bank personnel who open your envelope and post your deposit or payment. This can cause problems if a dispute arises over the amount of the deposit, particularly if cash is involved.

If you need to draw on your funds soon after making a deposit, ATM deposits may not be useful for you. Checks deposited into some ATMs are not subject to the 1987 law that strictly limits the "hold" banks can place on deposited funds. Your bank can place five-day holds on all checks deposited into any ATM it does not own. If a check you have deposited is not available for withdrawal in a timely fashion, you could write a check that you think is good, have it bounce, and damage your good credit. A telephone call to the bank's ATM customer service representative will confirm the availability of funds.

The availability of your money must be closely monitored when you transact business by electronic means. ATMs will give you a printed record of your withdrawal or deposit. Review it closely for accuracy, and keep it for verification with your bank statement. Enter the transaction in your checkbook immediately so you do not forget.

To make the most of ATMs, ask your bank for a listing of local ATM locations.

Tips to prevent problems with ATM transactions:

Preserve the card. Many cards are rejected by the ATM because they have been bent or demagnetized through use or abuse. If you tend to keep your wallet in your back pocket, you may eventually bend and break the card. If you find that ATMs give you trouble, consider keeping your card in a jacket pocket or card holder.

Keep the personal identification number (PIN) private. No matter how forgetful you may be, do not write down the access code anywhere, *especially not on the card.* If you simply cannot remember it, turn it into a bogus telephone number by adding a long-distance area code under a name in your address book.

Check the accounting on the spot. As you enter deposits with the machine, make sure you put the decimal point in the right place. Machines differ, so follow the instructions carefully. If you note an error, the ATM has a cancel function. Start over and check your receipt.

Retain your receipt and record the withdrawal. Since most of us are in a hurry when we use ATMs, we often neglect to write down the service fee, or even the withdrawal amount, in our checkbook. Do your accounting on the spot, or as soon as you return to your home or office.

Verify *ATM* activity on your monthly bank statement. All ATM activity is recorded according to amount, place, and time and date of transaction on your bank statement. Check your receipts against the bank's records.

What to Do if the ATM Gobbles Some of Your Money

In rare instances, an ATM will provide the wrong amount of cash. You may have told the machine to give you $100 and received $80 instead. If this happens, here is what you should do:

Use the customer courtesy phone. This will normally lead to a service call being placed to fix the machine. You will probably not get your money back right away, but the customer service representative will create a record of your complaint.

Document your trouble. Photocopy the receipt, write down the details of the problem, and contact the branch as soon as possible. Do not let any time pass needlessly.

Visit the bank's office as soon as possible. Explain your problem to the branch manager or assistant manager, showing the receipt you received. Most likely, the error will have shown up when ATM transactions were verified by the bank at the end of each day. If this has already happened, the bank should be prepared to credit your account for the disputed amount immediately, giving you a receipt documenting the credit. Otherwise, the bank should be able to tell you when the machine will be serviced next. If your problem has not been resolved within a few days, send a letter by certified mail to the branch manager.

What happens if someone uses your ATM card without your authorization? If you lose your card, or believe someone has stolen it, report it to your bank immediately. If you contact the bank within two business days after you learn of the loss, you will lose no more than $50 if someone has used your ATM card.

If you miss this two-day deadline, you can be held responsible for up to $500. Your liability can exceed these $50 and $500 ceilings, however, if the unauthorized withdrawals show up on your monthly statement but you fail to report them within 60 days after the statement is issued.

To help prevent someone from using your ATM card without your authorization, be sure to keep your PIN separate from the card. If you discover that your card has been lost or stolen, report it promptly. Do not worry if the loss or theft may have occurred weeks or months earlier. The $50 liability ceiling applies so long as you report the problem within two days after learning of it.

Review your statements carefully. If you see electronic withdrawals that you did not authorize, report them to your bank within 60 days.

❑   OTHER TYPES OF
ELECTRONIC FUNDS TRANSFERS

ATMs and telephone transfers are not the only kinds of electronic funds transfers available to you. Electronic payments and withdrawals can make your everyday banking easier if you protect yourself by managing your transactions well and keeping up-to-date records. Services your bank may offer include:

- Direct deposit of your paycheck or other recurring payments, such as retirement benefits
- Regular payments of your loans, which may actually save you some interest costs
- Preauthorized payments from your account for insurance premiums, mortgage payments, or utility bills
- Bill-payer services, which allow you to pay bills by touch-tone telephone
- Interbank transfer of funds
- Stock sales

☐ DIRECT DEPOSIT

If your employer offers direct deposit, consider this an attractive alternative; it is far superior to waiting in line to deposit your paycheck. Social Security checks can also be deposited this way. By arrangement with your bank, many kinds of regular payments, even child support or alimony payments, can be deposited directly into your account.

Direct deposit puts funds in your account when you are unable to get to the bank because of sickness, travel, or other circumstances. Your money begins to earn interest faster since banks do not place holds on funds directly deposited. With direct deposit, your money is also available for withdrawal faster.

The service fees, if any, for direct deposit programs vary from bank to bank and are usually borne by the employer. Be sure to enter the transaction in your checkbook as each direct deposit occurs.

☐ PREAUTHORIZED PAYMENTS OF RECURRING BILLS

With your onetime authorization, the bank can provide automatic payments each month or each payday of recurring bills such as car, mortgage, or other loan payments. Automatic withdrawals eliminate the need to write and mail checks to ensure these timely payments. This system of automatic payments protects your good credit rating and keeps you out of bank lines. It also facilitates personal financial planning by allowing you to concentrate on other investment interests rather than worrying about accounts payable.

You may be able to arrange for automatic transfers from your checking account to your loan account if they are with the same bank. That way, you will not have to worry about a lost or forgotten payment or deprive yourself of the use of your money several days before the monthly payments are due.

These services are arranged for you only if you ask for them. Unless you have just opened a new checking account, no one is likely to suggest them. Also, the cost of these services varies widely. Do not assume they are offered free or at a nominal cost. Most banks have a printed roster of transaction costs. Read it closely and have it explained to you before engaging in these various services.

Find out if the bank provides you with proof of payment should any concerns arise. Many banks send you a voucher by mail when the transfer occurs. Others document the transaction only on your bank statement, which may not arrive until several weeks after the transfer.

☐   **BANK·BY·MAIL**

Whether or not your bank advertises bank-by-mail or even lists it as a service, this is an option that allows you to stay out of line permanently and gives you the advantage of long-distance banking. Since interstate and regional banking are becoming more prevalent, bank-by-mail and bank-by-phone will take on increasing importance in the nineties.

An out-of-state bank may offer more attractive rates or lower service fees. You may wish to maintain financial ties with a resort area, your hometown, the town you just came from, or the town you'll be moving to next.

Obviously, when you bank long distance, it is more difficult to establish or maintain personal relations or to monitor the bank's activities or changes in staff, and there may be delays in handling special situations or resolving problems; you may have to incur long-distance telephone charges. Even if you can gain access to your cash from out-of-state banks through ATMs, you will probably face transaction fees of about a dollar.

If you choose to do most of your banking long distance by mail, it is also wise to maintain an active account locally. It is not any more unmanageable to have a local account and a long-distance account at two institutions than it is to have two accounts at the same bank. In any case, you will need the flexibility and convenience of immediate services, such as cashing checks, having an ATM card, and getting traveler's checks or notary services. You may even need a local safe deposit box. Most of these services are too cumbersome for bank-by-mail and the prospects of emergencies dictates a local banking relationship. It is also important to have a local bank reference when purchasing a car, getting a department store credit card, or making purchases by check.

Responding to Out-of-State Offers

An increasing number of banks invite mail business, and many bankers actively encourage long-distance relationships, particularly for the purpose of selling money-market accounts.

The new accounts representative at the bank will be happy to open an account for you by mail. He or she will send you all the forms, checks, deposit slips, and other relevant bank information so you can do your higher-interest banking for the cost of a first-class postage stamp. If the interest rate is high enough, any interest lost while your check is en route will not create a net loss. In any event, do not send cash through the mail. Mail can be easily lost and unaccountable. Instead, write a check.

Some financial magazines publish comparative lists of product and service offerings at banks across the country. Such analysis will allay your fears concerning the bank's solvency or the legitimacy of the claims and rates that are marketed by mail. You can also contact the National Technical Information Service at 703-487-4600, or write to NTIS, 5285 Port Royal Road, Springfield, VA 22161, to order a bank's "call report."

Other Banking and Financial Transactions by Mail

Your banker may be helpful in stopping payment on a check, transferring funds, or renewing a certificate of deposit or IRA through the mail. Call and ask for the appropriate forms to be sent to you. Remember that all bank activity done by mail must be documented, dated, and signed.

You Don't Need the Official Word

If your bank does not offer "bank-by-mail" as an official service, just send your deposit slip and the check to be deposited with the words "for deposit only" and your signature on the back to your key teller or branch manager. Photocopy both the check and deposit slip for your files and note the date you mail the deposit. Write a brief note that reads something like this:

> Dear Mr. Green:
> Enclosed please find my check for $900.00 to be immediately deposited to my savings account: #876 543 521. Please send my deposit receipt by return mail.
>
> Thank you,
> Mary Johnson

Your deposit will be made and your request honored.

❑   **BANK·BY·PHONE**

With WATTs, voice-mail systems, facsimiles, and touch-tone telephones, account information that once was available only from the teller is now available in your den or office. A growing number of banks across the country provide customers with a 24-hour telephone service that gives balance and check-clearing information.

One bank in Northern Virginia installed a system that allows a customer to gain access to account balances, recent deposit information, as well as the last ten checks cleared through his or her account by calling a toll-free number from a touch-tone phone.

FORGERY—
PUTTING YOUR MIND AT EASE

If you are worried about forgery through bank-by-mail, relax. The law is explicit and it is on your side. By law, the bank must have your signature on file, and it is required to file the actual signatures of *all* depositors to verify each and every check that clears the bank.

Since current technology cannot scan and compare each signature on every check economically, most banks have a set minimum balance for verification. Should a forged check of any size clear your account, notify the bank as soon as you discover it, and the bank will take responsibility for returning your funds. If you notify the bank by phone, follow up the call with a confirmation letter. Banks will either return the check to the bank that presented it or file a claim with their insurance company.

Forgery *is not* your fault; it *is* the bank's responsibility to compare signatures and verify identification. If you encounter a forgery, your bank will have you fill out appropriate forms. You then should ask to be reimbursed immediately.

Dial-a-Bank: EFT by Standard Touch-Tone Telephones

Banking by phone is available now through existing telephone equipment. Many institutions offer a bill-paying service in which customers can authorize a transfer from their checking accounts to pay specified bills. By prior arrangement with the bank, you can pay your mortgage, electric bill, phone bills, even department store bills by using your touch-tone phone.

The cost of installing these electronic systems has fallen significantly over the last few years. As a result, one bank has introduced services through touch-tone phones that enable customers to stop payment on checks, gain information on their last deposits, and find out which checks have cleared. Customers who arrange to pay bills by phone punch in the account number of the merchant being paid, followed by the dollar amount. The bank then sends the payment and subtracts the money from the customer's account.

The bank also offers discount long-distance services through an arrangement with AT&T that provides more than a 20-percent discount. To use the service, call the bank's ATM system by phone and punch in the telephone number you are trying to call, which is transmitted by AT&T. The bank handles the billing and includes the charges on your monthly statements.

Banks differ about whether they do or do not impose service charges on customers who bank by phone. In all cases, however, when dealing with a bank that provides such services, you are always paying for the service, either in the form of lower interest rates on deposits or as increased service charges in other areas. Before using these services, ask your bank representative how the bank recaptures the cost of providing the service. Banks do not, as some people believe, receive a commission for generating more business for the phone company.

Through an arrangement with Ticketmaster and other ticket outlets, some banks also offer price discounts and seat selection for entertainment events. In some cases, a computer will guide customers through seat selection before connecting them to a human operator for the actual ticket purchase.

Audio Response

Another available dial-a-bank setup is a system of audio response. As in the bill-paying program, the customer uses his or her touch-tone phone to gain access to accounts at the bank. An audio response system can permit a range of transactions, such as making balance inquiries, transferring funds between accounts, requesting applications, verifying that a check has cleared, and even withdrawing money. If your present bank has such a system in place, then perhaps you have received a roster of phone numbers through which you can gain access to various parts of the system.

Dial-a-Loan

A few banks now offer loan-by-phone programs, some of which *do not* require that applicants currently have accounts with them. A bank in Texas with over 60 locations accepts such telephone requests from anyone. When a loan officer receives the information for the loan application, he or she proceeds to collect credit information on the applicant. The bank advertises that in as little as 30 minutes, the applicant can find out if the loan has been approved.

Phones Made for Consumer Banking

New in the nineties, major New York–area banks and other financial institutions are developing modified telephones to facilitate bank-at-home services to the average consumer. The bank leases this enhanced telephone for $9.95 a month plus a onetime $49 fee. It can be used for home banking, making ordinary calls, storing telephone numbers, and automatic dialing.

Although banks want to position themselves in this new market, they are uncertain whether banking by phone will ever represent a large enough market to justify the expense of developing the hardware. The enhanced phone, which combines elements of a computer terminal and a telephone, has a program of "class services" that include voice messaging, gaining access to electronic directories, and caller identification. Since these telephone tellers are just being introduced, they probably won't begin to catch on in metropolitan areas for the next several years. However, the odds that your bank will soon offer some form of tele-banking are getting better each day.

☐ **BANK·BY·PERSONAL COMPUTER:**
GET OUT OF LINE, GO ON·LINE

Although personal computer industry enthusiasts had predicted that all types of "at-home" services would be in use by 1992, home banking by personal computer (PC) has yet to be profitable or successful for American financial institutions and has not been embraced by large numbers of consumers. Currently, there are only a couple hundred thousand users of PC-related banking in the United States and Canada, connected to fewer than 100 financial institutions.

As more people begin to use PCs at home, familiarity with modems increases, and the hassle of bank lines continues, banking-by-PC will undoubtedly command more consumer interest. Several interactive PC services offered by nationally reputable companies will ultimately increase the number of users to make PC-related banking the most effective, time-saving method for both consumers and institutions.

Monthly services are provided for both IBM and Apple computer systems, usually at $10 per month or less; once engaged, you will save not only time but also money and postage. A trip to the bank will become a rare occasion.

Banking from home requires a PC and modem, a communication software package, and a telephone line. If you bank by computer, you are actually making a telephone call, so be sure that your bank is within your local calling area or has a toll-free 800 number for you to use.

Some software packages are offered through major retail stores. One widely advertised service includes stock information and brokerage services, airline reservations, gift and grocery shopping, and an electronic encyclopedia for a flat monthly fee. Computerized banking is available *only* with an additional monthly fee to the bank. The software company's goal is to make banking services available to all users; consequently, the company is focusing its efforts on having its banking software offered by at least one bank in all major U.S. cities.

If you decide to bank by PC, some banks may give you their own customized software program as well as a modem. The bank fee to conduct computer banking is between $5 and $15 per month, which enables you to pay bills, reconcile your accounts, transfer funds, check balances, and issue stop-payment orders from your desk chair.

Instant Results

To make the system work, supply the bank with a list of payees such as your utilities, mortgage holder, loan companies, doctors, dentists, etc. The bank arranges with the creditors to receive your money by electronic transfer or by check, which the bank prepares and mails. The system almost always eliminates the "float": the minute you debit your account, the money is gone.

Be sure to print out hard-copy records of your computer transactions. At the end of the month, verify your bank statement against them. Bank statements can be printed daily, if you wish, to track the accuracy of your bank's interest payments. Most PC software packages contain a customer service or message option, so if you discover a mistake, you can call a human being via the computer to resolve the problem. Disputes are handled in much the same way as any other dispute you would have with the bank. Before signing up for such a program, however, it is wise to speak with other customers who bank by computer. If your bank cannot readily supply you with the names of some satisfied customers, proceed with caution.

❑   **WIRE TRANSFERS**

Many American banks allow you to "wire" money to another bank or financial institution. A wire transfer is a direct bank-to-bank transfer of funds between the Federal Reserve Bank accounts of two banks.

What makes wires so useful is that the receiving bank is required to credit your account immediately with the collected funds, which makes your deposit eligible for accruing interest.

Understandably, electronic funds transfer is exceptionally advantageous with large sums of money. Consider the cost of two weeks' lost interest on $100,000: about $290 at 7 percent interest compounded monthly. If you sell your home, come into an inheritance, or for some other reason expect to receive a large sum of money, be sure that your money is wired into an interest-bearing account on the day you sign the papers.

☐   **ONLY HALF THE BATTLE**

Knowing when your money is available to you is only half the battle. You must also carefully monitor the transactions themselves. Consider the case of the single parent who was refinancing her house after a divorce. Her objectives were to reduce her monthly mortgage payment to provide a higher standard of living for her children and to pay off the outstanding debts that she and her former husband incurred while they were married.

She requested that her settlement attorney wire the agreed-upon funds into her checking account. They were to be wired from the West Coast and be available in her attorney's account within 48 hours. On the third day, she called the settlement attorney's office to confirm that the funds had been transferred.

The answer was affirmative. She wrote and mailed out more than $10,000 worth of checks. On the fifth day, she called the bank to confirm that the money had been credited to her account. It was not. The bank assured her that the funds might be there but would not appear in her account electronically for 48 hours. Forty-eight hours later, on the seventh day, she called again and there was still no money in her account. At this point, the checks she had written were in the hands of some of her creditors. She was frantic. Tracing the transaction, she first called the settlement attorney. Although she was assured that the transfer had been completed, she insisted on seeing a facsimile copy of it. Upon review, she discovered that the settlement attorney's secretary had one digit wrong in her account number and that thousands of dollars had been deposited in another person's account.

She insisted that the secretary call the bank, redirect the funds to the proper account number, and instruct the branch manager of the error, ensure that no checks would bounce, and redirect the "lost" interest. To make the process fail-safe, she also called the bank and creditors herself and kept a record of the names, times, and transaction numbers for her files.

Be sure to follow up on electronic transactions, know your rights, and enforce them.

The Electronic Funds Transfer Act requires the bank to lay out in plain language the terms of its agreement with you in a printed disclosure. Read the disclosure, keep it, and refer to it when you have a concern.

The EFT Act, which is part of the Consumer Credit Protection Act, defines the basic rights, liabilities, and responsibilities of consumers who use these services.

The bank's printed disclosure should give you the following important information:

- Types of transfers you can make, the times you can make them, the cost, and any other restrictions on service
- Addresses and telephone numbers of places to write and call in case you encounter an error or lose your card or personal identification number (PIN)
- How to stop recurring payments that you have preauthorized, e.g., payments on car loans, mortgages, or utility bills

The bank must also supply you with documentation of every transaction.

More Errors in Store?

As electronic transfer services proliferate, identifying errors and resolving complaints may become more complex. Just as touch-tone telephones enable you to "dial" faster, they also have led to more errors in placing calls. Electronic banking aids will simplify many aspects of dealing with banks, but remember to record the date, time, and amount of each transaction when using a touch-tone service. That way, if there is a discrepancy, it can be rectified more easily.

Monitor your statements when they arrive. Ignoring or procrastinating in the reconciliation of your account statements has always been bad policy, more so now. Never assume accuracy.

If you do detect an error, act at once. The longer you delay, the less likelihood there is of correction. It will also be harder to reclaim interest and to avoid bad-check charges or other potential problems resulting from the error.

The EFT Act sets up special procedures for resolving errors related to the electronic transfer of funds. These rules apply whenever you think an error has occurred. For example, they apply when the ATM dispenses less cash than you requested, when an electronic debit that you did not make shows up on your monthly statement, or when a preauthorized electronic transfer of funds into your account does not occur as scheduled.

Under the act your bank is generally required to complete its investigation of the error within 10 business days after you report it. If the bank does not complete its investigation within 10 days, it must provisionally recredit your account for the disputed amount while it completes its investigation. In most cases, the absolute deadline for the bank to complete its investigation is 45 days after you report the error.

The bank is not required to recredit your account provisionally if it requests that you put your complaint in writing and you fail to do so. To preserve your right to provisional recrediting, your safest bet is to put your complaint in writing when you initiate the complaint process.

The EFT Act disclosure notice will give you the address where you must send your written complaint. If you cannot find the notice, just call the bank to get the correct address. Save a copy of your correspondence, along with any related documentation from the bank, and send your correspondence by certified mail.

Except where the dispute concerns an unauthorized withdrawal that appears on your monthly statement, the law does not set an outside time by which you must report an error to protect your interests. But, the faster you act, the faster the bank can act, and the more likely the bank will resolve the problem in your favor.

If the error involves a debit against your account that you did not authorize, you must report the error to the bank within 60 days after the debit appears on your statement. If you act within 60 days, your maximum liability for the unauthorized transfer is $50. If you delay beyond the 60 days, the bank will still be responsible, except for the $50 "deductible," for all of the unauthorized transfers that appear on the statement and for any that occur within the 60-day period after you receive the statement. However, the bank will be off the hook for any unauthorized withdrawals that occur after the 60 days expire and before you notify it that the withdrawals appearing on your statement are unauthorized.

When the bank completes its investigation, it must send you a written notice setting out the results. If it had provisionally credited your account for the disputed amount, but it decides that no error occurred, the bank will reverse the credit. Still, it must wait five business days before reversing the credit so you can deposit whatever funds may be necessary to compensate for the debit.

At this point, if you are convinced that an error did occur, you can appeal your case to higher authorities within the bank, to state or federal bank regulators, or to the courts.

❑   **OTHER WAYS**
                                 TO MAKE DEPOSITS CONVENIENTLY

A number of other approaches are available to minimize the duration of your visit to the bank:

- ❑ Use the night deposit box all day
- ❑ Bank during off-hours
- ❑ Make an appointment
- ❑ Make an after-hours appointment
- ❑ Designate a depositor
- ❑ Find an underused branch
- ❑ Use a private banker

Remembering the wide diversity in bank technology when you shop for a new bank, look for one that has on-line capabilities so that your deposits can be quickly transferred within branches of the same institution. This will minimize the number of transactions you conduct with your teller and provide immediate information for you at any branch when you need it.

❑   **USE THE NIGHT DEPOSIT BOX ALL DAY**

Whenever you have a deposit to make, even during midday, if the speed at which your deposit is posted is not of the essence, use the night deposit box. The night deposit is often located right next to the bank's ATM machine. If you have never used it before, you may have assumed it was only used for commercial accounts. Actually, any customer may use the night deposit box at any time. The bank will simply collect your deposit at the end of the day, post it the next morning, and mail you a deposit verification. Using the night box will reduce the amount of time you spend in the bank, while ensuring the security of your deposit.

❏ BANK DURING OFF·HOURS

If you cannot arrange direct deposit or if you receive income irregularly, there are predictable peak hours at any financial institution, which, if avoided, can reduce the time you will spend in the bank. Everyone is familiar with the rush to complete banking chores during lunch hour and near closing, in addition to the chaos and crush before the weekend. The day before any national holiday can also be a nightmare. Even with drive-in tellers, you can be in line for 15 minutes or more during these peak periods.

If you can, do your banking during midmorning or midafternoon, which are often quieter than opening, closing, or lunch hours.

❏ MAKE AN APPOINTMENT

If you plan to make a deposit, open a new account, buy a certificate of deposit, or take out a loan, call ahead for an appointment.

Ask for the person who is in charge of the service you require. Explain that you are very busy and cannot spend your time waiting for bank services. Offer to provide preliminary information over the phone so that the forms can be filled out in advance or have the forms mailed to you so that you can fill them out at home. Then all you have to do is sign them in the presence of a bank officer.

❏ MAKE AN AFTER·HOURS APPOINTMENT

If you have a large deposit or personal line of credit, the branch manager may be willing to meet with you after-hours to complete a transaction, so call for an appointment. To pick up a substantial check, some bankers may even come to your office or home.

❏ ## DESIGNATE A DEPOSITOR

Most of your banking does not require that you stand in line at the bank. Anyone you trust can make a deposit or withdrawal from your account with the proper forms and identification. Checks to be deposited need not be cosigned by whomever is depositing them. The check can simply be endorsed with your signature, the words "for deposit only," and your account number written on the back of the check.

Withdrawals by another person usually require two forms of identification in the name of the individual who has the account, such as a driver's license and a major credit card. In addition, the bank may require a letter of authorization from the account holder designating the other person as qualified to withdraw from the account. If the person making the withdrawal also has an account at the bank, he or she will have to cosign the check as well.

❏ ## FIND AN UNDERUSED BRANCH

Every major commercial bank or savings-and-loan institution has branches with a lower volume of customer traffic than others. Ask which branches have the lowest lobby traffic. A two-minute drive off your normal route may save you the hassle of a long wait in line.

❏ ## USE A PRIVATE BANKER

An annual income of $150,000 or assets exceeding $300,000 can get you a "personal banker" to do your bidding, to transfer money by telephone, open a CD, or perform other services. At some banks, when you are simply trying to cash a check, you can bypass the crowd and be taken to a quieter area while somone handles your transaction. The extent of such services often varies according to the amount in your account. One customer at a large Chicago bank needed a large sum after hours on Friday and was able to get a money order delivered to her home.

Consequently, depending on your bank, your net worth, and your own determination, you may experience no lines at all.

Bank Accounting: Bank Statements, the Float, Check Holds, and Grievance Procedures

5

T HE PREDICTIONS 20 YEARS AGO THAT THE COMPUTER WOULD create a cashless and paperless society have obviously proven inaccurate. The introduction of ATMs, home computers, and bank-by-phone services have merely made accounts more accessible to the consumer and increased the number of transactions. Computers have not made banking any more free of errors, and most banking consumers do not handle appreciably less paper.

Your bank statement provides the *bank's version of your monthly transactions*. Comparing it to your checkbook record provides a simple system to protect your finances. Moreover, in case of an Internal Revenue Service audit, individuals must keep financial records related to their tax returns for at least three years, unless fraud is proven; then there is no time limit.

☐ ## CAN YOU DECIPHER
THE BANK'S MONTHLY STATEMENT?

Most banks send a monthly statement on your checking and savings accounts. Some banks consolidate the two. The statement is the basic documentation and communication vehicle the bank provides you; consequently, you need to be comfortable in understanding the statement you receive.

As a rule, bank statements list all transactions made on the account, including deposits and checks written and cleared during the previous month, up to a cut-off date. They include applicable interest paid and any service charges incurred. Cleared and "returned" checks are enclosed if that is your bank's policy.

It is not possible to reconcile your account if you neglect to record every transaction in your checkbook. The statement may include a worksheet on the back to "balance" your checkbook. It is easier to make copies of this worksheet than to keep turning it over to refer to the bank's information. See the sample form on pages 74 and 75.

☐ ## VERIFY INTEREST
ON YOUR DEPOSITS AND BALANCES

The bank must credit your deposit according to a schedule established by law. Your bank statement will include the dates that your deposits are credited. The bank pays interest on the balance according to set policy. Make sure it is based on your average daily balance. This policy is included in the paperwork you receive when you open an account and includes in-person, mail, ATM, and EFT transactions. Read the fine print.

Pay attention to the institution's declared right to change the interest rate being paid to investors. Certificates of deposit pay a fixed interest rate for a contracted period of time. The penalties for withdrawals before the maturity date are significant (such as the loss of three months' worth of interest). Be aware of the penalties before making an investment.

BALANCE YOUR BANK STATEMENT

STEP 1. GETTING READY

Sort all withdrawal receipts, checks, or drafts returned with your statement by date and number. Compare all these returned items with the entries you made in your account register. Also, compare other withdrawal items shown on the statement with your recorded entries. Next, compare your deposit entries with deposits shown on your statement. Put a check (✓) beside each matching check or other withdrawal and deposit entry.

Locate the last item in your account register that you have checked off, either a deposit or a check/withdrawal. Draw a line under the balance following this entry. Deal only with items above this line for steps 2 and 3.

Enter the balance here. $_____

STEP 2. WITHDRAWALS

List any checks or other withdrawal items in your register that you did not check off.

ITEM	AMOUNT

Enter the total here. $_____ +
Add total to the balance from above. $_____

List any checks or other withdrawal items shown on this statement but not in your account register.

ITEM	AMOUNT

(Also enter them in your
account register.)

Enter the total here. $_____ —

Subtract total from the balance $_____
above.

STEP 3. DEPOSITS/
INTEREST

ITEM	AMOUNT

Add any deposits or
interest shown on your
statement but not in your
register. (Also enter them $_____ +
in your account register.) $_____

Subtract any deposits in your account $_____ —
register that you did not check off. $_____

The final total should be the same as $_____
the closing balance shown on your
statement.

If your total does not agree with the closing balance on
your statement:

1. Check your addition and subtraction.
2. Be sure you have accounted for all items in
   your account register.
3. Verify that you entered all interest and
   other items from your last statement.

NOTE: The next time you balance your account you
may want to use a different color ink or substitute a **X**
for a **✓**. This alternating method will help you determine which items belong to your current statement.

☐ TAKE ADVANTAGE OF THE FLOAT

Bank accounting is different from the accounting principles that consumers and small businesses use. By giving loans, banks earn interest. Because your deposits are simply held by the bank, but not owned by the bank, your cash is actually treated as a liability on the bank's books. When the bank gives you a loan, the amount of the loan is counted as an asset on the bank's books.

Suppose the bank lends you $15,000 and dispenses it in the form of a cashier's check. You sign the papers, thereby increasing the assets of the bank, while so far no money has actually changed hands. The bank has temporarily "created" $15,000. That week you shop for a car. Seven days later, you choose the model you want and give the cashier's check to the dealer, who deposits it in his or her bank. Depending on the day of the week, it can take nearly seven days for the bank to honor the check. You are paying interest on the loan from day one, yet the bank has had use of that money for two weeks. At 10 percent, that means $58.68 is earned by the bank on one loan even before it has paid out the amount of the loan. Consider how many loans your bank makes in a month and its resulting profits.

Since the bank can hold your deposits for up to five business days on an out-of-town check, your money is available to the bank at an interest rate usually 4 to 6 points higher than what you will be paid. Float adds to their revenues, especially if they charge you for having drawn against uncollected funds, often whether they pay or return the check you have drawn.

Although the vast majority of checks written in this country are valid, the check-holding policy is so ingrained in the institutions, changes now are possible only through consumer pressure on the institutions themselves and through Congress.

Make the Float Work for You

If your regular source of income is a paycheck, work with the bank where your check originates if possible. That way, your deposit will be credited immediately as an "in-house" transfer of funds. You can also cash your paycheck and make an immediate cash deposit.

By banking in the same check processing region as your paycheck you eliminate the permissible five-business-day holding period. Direct deposit (or electronic transfer) puts your money to work for you within 24 hours. More companies offer this option these days.

Also, use your ATM to best advantage. The policy for automatic teller machines at most banks is to credit the amount on the first business day after the deposit. By doing the teller's work yourself rather than waiting for the bank to open again, depositing your check on Saturday afternoon will cause it to be credited and available to you on Monday. If you had made the deposit with a teller late on Monday, it might not have been available to you until Wednesday after 2:00 P.M. Check your bank's policy to be sure.

Pay Your Bills When They Are Due, Not Before

Write the due dates for your bills on a planning calendar. Note the dates of your deposits. Date the checks the day the payment is due. Mail the checks to arrive on the due date. If there is a discrepancy, note the date the check was deposited. On an out-of-state check, the funds should not clear for five business days. On an in-state check, the funds should not clear for two business days. This will assure that your average daily balance is as high as possible and that your bills are paid on time.

Pay Your Utilities at the Bank on the Day Before They Are Due

The payment is credited on the date of your receipt, but the bank will not debit your account for 24 hours because of the computer ledgers. Most banks have a cutoff time of 2:00 P.M. Over a year's time, these extra balances over extra days can add up to a significant amount.

☐ AVAILABILITY OF FUNDS AND THE LAW

As a consumer, you need to know when you can get your money. Excessive holds placed on deposited checks delay when you can draw on those funds.

Before Congress passed the Expedited Funds Availability Act in 1987, some banks placed holds on deposits sometimes exceeding two weeks. You were prevented from withdrawing your money while the bank earned interest on it. The new law requires financial institutions to make funds available according to deadlines based on the type of check and the location of the paying bank in relation to your own. The final schedule went into effect in 1990.

Based *strictly* on the tenets of the law, here is a quick guide for withdrawing funds based on when your deposits are made. Remember that the following need only represent the worst-case scenario. If you are known by your bank, and have active accounts there, the bank may make your money available more quickly.

When You Can Get Your Money

Available the next business day after a deposit:
Cash
U.S. Treasury checks
State and local government checks (same state)
Checks drawn on the same bank
First $100 of any check
Cashier's checks
Certified checks

Teller's checks
Depository checks
All wire transfers

Available no later than the second business day after a deposit (for example, if you deposit funds on Monday, they must be available on Wednesday):

> All checks drawn on local institutions (within the same Federal Reserve Bank check-processing region as yours), which generally means same city and maybe same state.

Available no later than the fifth business day after a deposit (for example, if you deposit funds on Monday, they must be available Saturday, if the bank is open then, or the following Monday):

> All checks drawn on nonlocal financial institutions. (Banks in Hawaii, Alaska, U.S. Virgin Islands, and Puerto Rico can take an extra business day to credit checks drawn on banking institutions not inside their geographic borders.) The regulations do not apply to checks into new accounts for the first 30 days after the account is opened or checks greater than $5,000.

The law offers considerable protections not previously available. However, if a bank decides to be difficult, for example, you might not be able to withdraw $100 this afternoon, even though you deposited $100 in cash that same morning. You would then have to wait until the next business day.

Their Error or Yours?

Before you get upset with your bank for a transaction error, check to make sure that you are not at fault. Here are some of the most frequent errors made by consumers that can be detected on a bank statement:

- □ Failure to record a check
- □ Failure to record an ATM transaction
- □ Failure to record the ATM service charge
- □ Addition or subtraction error in check record
- □ Failure to record maintenance or service charges levied by the bank
- □ Entering a deposit or withdrawal twice
- □ Entering a deposit in the check record on the wrong date
- □ Writing checks on a deposit too quickly
- □ Failure to calculate interest paid on average daily balance
- □ Failure to detect a lost or uncashed check

Be sure to note the terms of your account. Many accounts call for the correction of errors within a certain time frame, such as 30 or 60 days.

The most frequent errors made by banks include the following:

- □ Deposits credited on the wrong day
- □ Interest credited on the wrong day
- □ Checks returned for insufficient funds after a sufficient deposit
- □ Service charges levied on an account incorrectly
- □ Deposit or interest credited to the wrong account
- □ Errors in data entry
- □ Simple math errors

All these errors are detectable on your monthly bank statement. Regardless of the type of transaction and the type of equipment used, bank errors can occur occasionally. If you have been wronged in any way, proceed on the premise that it was an honest mistake—the bank has plenty of legal ways to make money from you.

☐ GRIEVANCE PROCEDURES

If a mistake has been made on your account, you should register a complaint. If you don't then get action, you might consider informing several decision makers of the problem. Do not overreact to a $4.50 miscue. If the bank is incorrectly computing the interest on your bank credit card in direct violation of its advertised rates, and nobody seems interested in correcting it, you have an issue that higher management should know about. Keep a file of names, dates, conversations, copies of letters sent and received, and any other appropriate materials.

Gather all your facts and write a clear and concise letter of complaint, including *what you expect* in terms of resolution. Request compensation for lost interest and the return of any fees incurred by mistake. Be persistent. If you encounter rudeness or feel neglected, add this information to your complaint.

Write a letter of complaint. Hard copy gets far more attention than conversation. Type a simple letter that consists of the following elements:

◻ A definition of the problem
◻ The time, date, location, transaction number, etc., of the problem or error
◻ If relevant, include a history of your attempts to solve the problem. Name those with whom you attempted to resolve it and any associated problems with personnel or procedure.
◻ Include a brief history of your relationship with the bank, including length of time as a customer, other accounts, and services used.
◻ State the time frame in which you expect the problem to be corrected.
◻ Include your full name, address, account number, and home and work telephone numbers so that you can be reached for further information.

▫ Finally, state your next action if your complaint is not addressed.

Send a copy of the letter to the head of the department where the error occurred, the branch manager, the bank president, and the board of trustees. Since board members tend to be executives in their own industry, send your letter of complaint to them at their business address. On the envelope, write "Personal and Confidential." This will reduce the possibility of the letter being seen only by an administrative assistant. For faster results, send your letters of complaint by registered mail. That way, a signature is required.

Someone may call. When you receive a telephone call, ask for the correction and compensation you believe is fair and just. The caller may be at a high level and will assign a lower-level manager to resolve your complaint. Even though you may have previously addressed a verbal complaint to the lower-level manager, he or she will now have incentive to see it through to a satisfactory resolution.

You may prefer to set up an appointment with a customer relations or public affairs director, or a senior officer at the bank. On this or any other grievance, you can also use your relationship with the branch manager to resolve the dispute. Bring your paperwork with you.

If the complaint is not resolved after visiting a bank official and you feel that your rights have been violated, suggest that you will be pursuing the issue through one of the following legal or regulatory means: small claims court (restrictions vary from state to state), arbitration, appealing directly to a federal agency, or calling on your congressional representative.

Still no satisfaction? If you have not received a satisfactory resolution of the problem within the bank's structure, write to the Federal Reserve Board's Office of Consumer Affairs. This office resolves problems regarding its state-chartered members of the

Federal Reserve System. If your problem is outside its jurisdiction, it will refer you to the appropriate federal agency. These may include:

▫ Federal Trade Commission
▫ Federal Deposit Insurance Corporation
▫ National Credit Union Administration
▫ Comptroller of the Currency
▫ Office of Thrift Supervision

Write to:

Board of Governors, Federal Reserve System
Office of Consumer and Community Affairs
20th and C Streets, N.W.
Washington, DC 20551
(202) 452-3946

Other complaint options include your state government's consumer protection agency, your local better business bureau or your area's consumer group, newspaper, and television or radio "action hotlines."

Most banks will go to extremes to avoid negative publicity. Let them know how far you are willing to go and the bank may find a way to resolve your claim more quickly.

After your complaint is resolved, write a thank-you letter to anyone who interceded on your behalf. This is a two-fold opportunity. It tells the senior officer of the bank that he or she is dealing with a person who knows how to say thank you as well as how to complain. It also enables the person who directly handled your complaint to get to know you and have more respect for your financial affairs in the future. Now that he or she knows you will not let a problem lie unresolved, the banker will make every effort to make sure you are a satisfied customer who has no problems at his level.

❏ CREDIT CARD ERRORS

If you discover an error on your monthly credit card statement, your right to dispute the bill is protected by the Fair Credit Billing Act. The law covers mistakes on your periodic statements; charges you did not make or charges made by an unauthorized person; charges billed incorrectly with the wrong amount, date, or description; and charges for services or goods that you did not receive or accept, or which were not delivered as agreed.

The law also covers failure to credit your account for returned goods, accounting errors, billings for which you request an explanation or proof of purchase, and failure to mail or deliver a billing statement to your current address. To protect your rights to dispute the bill without jeopardizing your credit rating, however, you must make your complaint *in writing* to the credit card issuer within 60 days after the bill was mailed to you.

The complaint must include your name, address, and account number, an explanation of the error, and the total dollar amount in dispute. You are responsible for paying the amount of the bill not in dispute.

The credit card issuer then has 90 days to answer. It may either correct the error or explain why it believes the bill is correct. If the dispute is not resolved, you must notify the merchant in writing within 10 days after receiving the credit card issuer's explanation. At that point, the merchant may report you to a collection agency or a credit bureau, stating that you have disputed the bill.

A recent glitch by Visa's main computer system, for example, billed some customers twice for the same purchase. The malfunction at a California facility that processes Visa and some MasterCard credit card charges transmitted data twice to the banks. Although the error was caught by Visa's in-house monitoring system, only the bank was notified; the customers and merchants were not. Later, all customers involved received a corrected statement and the associated finance charges were removed.

6

Borrowing Money from the Bank

THE CURRENT PROBLEMS OF COMMERCIAL LENDING FOLLOWING on the heels of the savings-and-loan crisis will cast a long shadow throughout the nineties. It is understandable that bankers are worried. Their reputation for being a safe haven for personal savings has been damaged. Moreover, Americans are saving less now than they did in previous decades and borrower defaults are on the rise.

In 1988, 1 out of every 178 households (totaling nearly 600,000) declared bankruptcy, nearly twice the rate since 1980. In 1990, the figure grew to 718,000, or 1 out of every 153 households. The average amount of debt associated with each of these filings has increased as well. In 1988, the average outstanding debt was $37,400; in 1990, it increased to $40,000. By 1995, the number of personal bankruptcies declared annually may top 800,000 with an average outstanding debt exceeding $50,000 per filing.

Statistics like these, combined with the large proportion of commercial real estate loans in the portfolios of many financial institutions, make bankers nervous.

With the advent of bank cards in the sixties, consumer credit has been easily available without the interaction that formerly went along with borrowing money. In addition, many consumers have relationships with several institutions across the country. More people, however, find themselves having difficulty making payments on multiple cards. In short, it is getting easier to miss a payment, which can damage your credit rating.

While credit is now offered to broad segments of the population, more consumers face complex decisions about credit use without anyone to counsel them. As a result, they are often inadequately prepared to address financial decisions in such areas as applying for home equity loans, consolidating loans, or choosing a fixed or variable rate mortgage. Against this backdrop, consumers at all income levels and backgrounds are experiencing credit problems today. Bankers find that they need to be more careful in extending credit, while consumers are learning that they need to be more judicious in using it. If lenders and borrowers do not exercise greater prudence, ultimately bank regulation will have to be tightened to the point where people will face very stringent standards that greatly reduce their access to credit.

❏　　　　　THE AMERICAN DREAM PREVAILS

A home is the single largest investment that most people make. Though home ownership is still the American dream, to many consumers it is just a dream. Mortgage origination tumbled 22 percent between 1986 and 1989 and is expected to decrease further in what is currently a soft real estate market.

The median cost of a starter home in the United States today exceeds $90,000. To qualify for a mortgage on such a home, you would need an income of about $36,000. By contrast, the median income nationally is $34,000. Loans backed by the Federal Housing Administration (FHA) will cover homes up to a price tag of $124,875. In more than 80 cities across the country, the median price for a home is above the FHA limit, eliminating that alternative for a large number of households.

To afford a $125,000 home, you would need a down payment of $25,000, an annual income above the national median, and little debt. Your monthly mortgage payments at 9.25 percent interest for 30 years would be about $822. Add taxes, insurance, energy, and local fees, and your fixed housing cost would exceed $1,000 a month. However, these numbers presume going with conventional, rather than FHA, financing.

Mortgages Are Still Being Written

Despite the bad news, mortgage loans are made every day. Commercial banks of late have originated more residential mortgages than savings-and-loans. In general, mortgage loans are available from commercial banks, savings-and-loans, credit unions, and mortgage brokers. You can get the mortgage loan you want, but recognize that the process may be time-consuming. Establishing good credit is the first step.

□ ESTABLISH A GOOD CREDIT HISTORY

As simple as it sounds, if you want to get loans faster and easier, pay your bills on time. This ranks high on the list from a lending officer's point of view. Paying on time is particularly important during the 12 months prior to seeking a mortgage loan. Suppose you own your current residence and want to buy a more expensive home. Your recent payment history will heavily influence your ability to get a larger mortgage.

Surprisingly, many people make late mortgage payments inadvertently. Paying late diminishes your creditworthiness when you apply for any kind of loan, and it costs you money. Late payments carry late-payment fees or charges of 1.5 percent per month or higher, equal to an 18 percent annual charge. Depending on the complexity of your household and time constraints, there are several systems that work.

One busy executive has a bill calendar separate from her personal planning calendar on the wall of her home office. At the beginning of each year, she notes the due date of each payment, including personal property taxes, Internal Revenue Service prepayments, vacation deposits, etc., four business days preceding the due date. She then writes the checks and mails them on that date, maximizing the interest on her account.

❑   ## KEEP ABREAST OF YOUR CREDIT REPORT

Consumers Union offers these tips for dealing with credit bureaus:

- ❑ Check your credit report on a routine basis at each of the three major credit reporting agencies—CBI (Equifax's credit report division), the Trans Union Corporation, and TRW Information Services Division. Their addresses and phone numbers should be in the white pages of your phone book.
- ❑ Find out whether your state has a ceiling on the price that can be charged for credit bureau reports. Otherwise it can cost up to $60, $120 if married.
- ❑ If a dispute is resolved in your favor, make sure that your credit bureau report is corrected accordingly.
- ❑ If a dispute is not resolved in your favor, add a statement to your credit file explaining your position on the accuracy of the information.

Recently, credit bureaus have come under attack for having inaccurate data in their files. In 1991, a small study by Consumers Union showed that 48 percent of the credit reports it reviewed had inaccurate information in them.

Many consumers never think about their credit report until they are notified by a lender that they have been turned down for a loan because their credit report was not favorable. This is a mistake.

A credit bureau is an information center where data about you and your finances are assembled. It attempts to offer a written history of how you pay bills and conveys your payment patterns over the history of each account. Creditors from credit card to finance companies provide information on you and your accounts. In exchange, they receive information from the bureau on new and other accounts and how those account holders handle debt.

If you are able to pay your bills on time, have no payment disputes, and have not filed for bankruptcy or had other judgments levied against you, chances are your report reflects what is called "good credit."

If you are unable to pay a bill on time, explain your situation to your creditor in writing. Ask the creditor to work with you to establish a reasonable payback plan. Although your credit rating is still in jeopardy, it will increase the likelihood of being granted a mortgage or loan in the future should your financial situation improve.

☐ THE CONTENTS OF YOUR CREDIT REPORT

At the credit bureau, your file will contain personal information, such as your birth and married names, age, spouse's name, number and ages of dependents, recent addresses and how long you have lived at these addresses, whether you own or rent, your Social Security number, and a list of financial institutions, companies, and merchants that have issued you credit.

If complete, your file will list creditors, such as American Express, Visa, MasterCard, store and gasoline station cards, car loan companies, and mortgage companies. It will also list the amount of credit granted and the terms, the amount you owe, the amount in arrears, and how late your payments were (30-60-90 days).

There is a separate column for remarks that include information on whether you paid as agreed or prepaid a loan. If you made late payments for a reason, such as the loss of a job, a divorce, a serious illness, the death of a spouse, or other life-changing event that affected your cash flow, they too may be noted on your file.

The file will also contain information regarding lawsuits, judgments, garnishments, and other legal actions for seven years preceding the date of the report. Bankruptcies stay in the file for ten years. The credit report will list a married female's credit history under both her married and maiden names, if different.

❏   **DANCING WITH CREDIT BUREAUS**

If you apply for credit and are rejected because of your most recent credit report, the lender must tell you the source of the report—that is, the credit bureau that supplied the information. Within 30 days, you should obtain copies of your report from all three major credit bureaus, including the source that the lender provides. Technically, you only have a right to get your report without charge from the lender's source. In actual practice, however, you can often get all three reports for free, and credit bureaus will often allow you 60 days to request copies.

When you receive the reports, check for inaccuracies. If important past loans that you have paid on time are missing, call the lender who gave you the loan to obtain documentation that can be added to your report. If you have recently relocated, request that the credit report from your former home region be forwarded to the bureau in your new area, though it will probably be the same or affiliated with the bureau from the old region.

If there is an error, write immediately to correct it, using the dispute form that is normally attached to your report. Rather than having the credit bureau serve as a passive, dispassionate collector of data, you can actively use the bureau to protect your good rating. The Fair Credit Reporting Act gives you the right to insert a statement of 100 words or less to explain any credit problem. The bureau is obligated to attach it to your credit report, along with any pertinent documentation, such as photocopies of letters, canceled checks, and financial statements. Be sure to keep the originals for your files. You can then ask the bureau to verify your version of events with the past lender. Cleaning up your credit report is good preparation for a quick turnaround on a mortgage loan.

❑ **REVIEWING YOUR CREDIT REPORT IN ADVANCE**

Do not allow a mistake to be the cause of the loss of your dream home. If you know the bank or S&L where you will be applying for a mortgage or other credit within the next 12 months, *now* is the time to review your credit report for mistakes or "flags" that might cause your loan to be turned down. Ask for the addresses of the bureaus the lender uses to obtain consumer credit files so you can obtain copies of your report in advance. You may do the same with a local merchant, such as a car dealership or department store. Unless you have been denied credit within the past 30 days, you will have to pay a fee.

❑ **PREPARING A PERSONAL FINANCIAL STATEMENT**

When you apply for a mortgage loan, you will be asked to provide a personal financial statement. Some banks will attempt to learn from this statement everything they want to know before deciding whether or not you qualify for the loan you requested. Others will require additional information and documentation, such as pay stubs, income projections, W-2s, and more.

A personal financial statement is simply a description of what you have and what you owe. Your assets could include the dollar value of your savings, checking, certificates of deposit, and IRAs; personal property, such as cars, jewelry, antiques, art, furnishings, and boats; and investments such as stocks and bonds, real estate, trust funds, and other items of worth. Liabilities are debts to credit card companies, existing balances on mortgages, student loans, car loans, and other monies owed.

List your bank accounts, account numbers, addresses, and all other pertinent information. The value of your car is its blue book value (available at your bank or library). Jewelry, antique, or art appraisals should be photocopied and attached. Be honest about your liabilities. List the total amounts due, to whom they are due, and your monthly payments.

ASSETS	LIABILITIES
Everything you own with cash value.	What you owe: your debts.
CASH Money you have on hand. Include cash at home, today's checking and savings account balances. $___	ACCOUNTS PAYABLE Total balance of what you owe today on bills for goods and services (such as doctor bills) and credit card and store accounts. A credit card company or store usually lists the account's total balance due on the monthly statement mailed to you. If you do not have these records, contact the credit department of firms where you have accounts. $___
STOCKS, BONDS, OTHER SECURITIES U.S. Savings Bonds, Treasury issues, other money market and stock market investments. Check your records for documentation of current holdings. Current market value for some types of securities may be	

ASSETS	LIABILITIES

ASSETS

found in newspaper financial pages; for others, contact your broker. $____

CASH SURRENDER VALUE LIFE INSURANCE Investment or equity built up in your whole or straight life insurance policy; not face value. (Term life insurance has no cash surrender value.) Find the cash surrender value from the chart on your policy. $____

ACCOUNTS RECEIVABLE Money owed to you for goods and/or services. Check your files for items outstanding. $____

NOTES RECEIVABLE Money owed to you and documented by promissory notes. Check your records for the balance of any note due you. $____

LIABILITIES

CONTRACTS PAYABLE Total remaining balance on installment credit contracts for goods such as a car, furniture, appliances, or services of someone working for you under contract. To figure the total amount due, multiply your monthly payment by the number of months remaining on the contract. $____

NOTES PAYABLE Total balance due on cash loans, both secured and unsecured. Contact the office where you received the loan if you do not have these figures. $____

TAXES Federal and state income or property taxes due as of today (including any past due taxes). Do not list property taxes if they are automatically included

ASSETS

REBATES/REFUNDS
Money owed to you for refundable deposits, sales or tax refunds or rebates. Check your files for receipts and current 1040 income tax form. $____

AUTOS/OTHER VEHICLES   Trucks, trailers, mobile homes, motorcycles, campers, boats, and airplanes. Vehicle dealers and some libraries carry price catalogues. $____

REAL ESTATE   Any land and/or structures affixed to land. Also, legal rights you may have to resources in the land; growing crops, water, minerals, etc. For an estimate of the current market value, you may want to contact a local real estate agent or hire a professional appraiser. $____

VESTED PENSION
Nonforfeitable rights

LIABILITIES

with your mortgage payments or income taxes if they are automatically withheld. Self-employed people should include any Social Security taxes due. Check your income tax or property tax statements. $____

REAL ESTATE LOANS
Balance you owe on deeds of trust (mortgages) on your property. Contact the office where you received the loan if you do not have these figures. Also list any liens on property that you are liable for and must pay. $____

OTHER LIABILITIES
Court-ordered judgments of payments you must make, lawsuit settlements, past due accounts, etc. $____

TOTAL LIABILITIES $____

ASSETS

to benefits you accumulate after a certain time under your employer's pension plan. To find the current amount of your benefits, you must submit a written request to your employer or plan administrator. $___

KEOGH OR INDIVIDUAL RETIREMENT ACCOUNT
Available to those without employer pension plans or the self-employed. Record your account balance. $___

OTHER ASSETS
Any property other than real estate that has cash value, estimated in terms of what it is worth today. To find an item's value, check classified ads for comparable items or get estimates from dealers or special appraisers. $___

LIABILITIES

CONTINGENT LIABILITIES   Debts you may or may not come to owe sometime in the future. If you co-signed a note and the other signer does not pay, you may be responsible for paying the debt. If a suit is pending against you, you may be liable to pay a settlement. $___

ASSETS		LIABILITIES	
Home furnishings/ household goods/ appliances	$___	**NET WORTH** Your assets less your liabilities.	
Hobby/sports equipment	$___	**ASSETS**	$___
Art/antiques/ collections/jewelry/ furs	$___	**LESS LIABILITIES**	$___
Trade/professional tools and equipment	$___	**NET WORTH**	$___
Livestock/pets for show or breeding	$___	To check your figures, make sure:	
Trusts/patents/ memberships/ interest in estate	$___	Assets − Liabilities = Net Worth	
Interest in business/ farm/commercial operation/ investment club. (Any whole or part ownership.)	$___		
TOTAL ASSETS	$___		

In advance of your application, your realtor or mortgage broker can help you determine the steps to facilitate loan approval. For example, you may want to pay off one car or several credit cards to reduce your fixed monthly payments. The more work you do in preparing for your mortgage application, the quicker the bank can decide if you qualify.

❏   **HOW MUCH**
CAN YOU AFFORD TO BORROW?

Lenders look at the amount of down payment you are able to make, the size of the loan, and any other refinancing plans. For the lender, obviously, the more money you can provide for a down payment, the safer the loan. Ideally, the bank would loan no more than 70 percent of the value of the home, but many banks loan up to 90 percent and some will go as high as 95 percent.

Until recently, lenders considered your total annual income and were willing to loan you two and one-half times that figure. In other words, if you made $40,000, you could be granted a loan of up to $100,000. Depending on the type of loan and terms, you would pay roughly a little under a $1,000 a month on the mortgage. This has changed, however. Financial institutions now consider your outstanding debts, such as car payments, credit card bills, revolving charge accounts, and the like.

Your monthly housing expenses should not be more than 28 percent of your income before taxes and all your monthly housing expenses plus outstanding monthly obligations should not exceed 36 percent. If your expenses are higher than that, even if you make $40,000 annually, you would not be able to get a $100,000 loan.

Viewed another way, your ability to pay a monthly mortgage is calculated by most lenders as being equal to 28 percent of your monthly income before taxes. So, if you earn $3,333 per month before taxes ($40,000 annually) lenders would figure that you could pay $933 a month on a mortgage without discomfort.

If your expenses and obligations exceed these margins you will have to meet strong compensating conditions to get the loan you want. Plainly stated, if you are shopping for a mortgage, any outstanding debt will stand against your qualifying for a loan. Which is why it is important to pay off those revolving credit accounts and bank cards before you apply.

ESTIMATING
YOUR MAXIMUM HOUSE PAYMENT

Financial institutions traditionally use both of the calculations below to determine the amount of house payment you can qualify for. By filling out both parts of this worksheet, you will be able to estimate roughly your maximum house payment.

A. INCOME RATIO
The general rule with this calculation is that *your total house payment* (principal, interest, taxes, and insurance) should not exceed 28 percent of your total gross monthly income.

Total gross monthly income $_____
(Yours and any co-borrower's before taxes)

Multiply by 28 percent   × .28

Estimated maximum monthly house payment $_____
(principal, interest, taxes, and insurance)

B. TOTAL DEBT RATIO
The general rule here is that your *total debt payments* (house payment, loans, credit cards, and other debt obligations) should not exceed 36 percent of your total gross monthly income.

Total gross monthly income $_____
(Yours and any co-borrower's before taxes)

Multiply by 36 percent   × .36

Multiply by 36 percent ⟶ $\times .36$

Equals your total debt ceiling $= (A)$ $\$_____$

Total of your existing monthly debt payments $= (B)$ $\$_____$

(Include all debts: car loan, credit cards, child support, alimony, etc.)

Subtract (B) from (A), equals your **Estimated maximum monthly house payment** $\$_____$

(principal, interest, taxes, and insurance)

❑ **APPLYING FOR A MORTGAGE LOAN**

If you have established a good credit history and know that you have a sound credit report from your local credit bureau, you have completed the fundamental steps on the way to getting a mortgage loan.

Loan officers consider five items when assessing your loan request:

- ▫ Character
- ▫ Capacity
- ▫ Capital
- ▫ Collateral
- ▫ Conditions

Character   This first test often includes a personal history as well as a credit history. It is conceivable that those collecting

LOAN TERMINOLOGY

INTEREST
What you pay the bank for the use of its money, expressed as a percentage of the amount borrowed.

POINTS
An added onetime payment to the financial institution. One point is usually 1 percent of the mortgage amount. Points can be added to the loan or paid up front. Though banks present them as a take-it-or-leave-it matter, points are negotiable.

ORIGINATION FEES
These include everything from legal expenses to credit reports, title searches, property appraisals, termite inspections, courier fees, long-distance charges, and more. It is not unreasonable to ask for one point lower or to have most origination fees on your loan elimi-

information for the bank will ask your work associates or neighbors a few brief questions about you. Remember, too, that how you fill out the application, converse on the phone, and otherwise conduct yourself provide a strong message to the loan officer about your character.

Capacity This is a measure of your financial ability to manage the loan in the future. The best of intentions will not pay your mortgage payment. If you have a position of considerable responsibility at work, a regular, reliable income, and a good job history, your capacity to pay back the loan will appear strong.

Capital The financial resources you have to help you make payments if unexpected expenses come up, or if you suffer a set-

nated. In a slow housing market, you have a higher possibility for success.

REAL ESTATE COMMISSIONS
A typical commission is 6 percent, although some brokers discount commissions. The seller pays the commission in all but a few cases. Ask your real estate agent about commissions before listing your home for sale.

INSURED LOANS (VA AND FHA)
To help citizens realize the American dream of home ownership, the U.S. government has two insurance plans that guarantee repayment to the bank should the borrower default. VA (Veterans Administration) assists veterans of the armed forces and FHA (Federal Housing Administration) has programs for nonveterans. The local offices of VA and FHA have information on the criteria for these programs.

back in your earnings, are considered your capital. Your annual income, current and long-term obligations, and net worth are among the factors that play a role in influencing the loan officer.

Collateral The package of material things you possess to back up the bank's confidence that you can pay back the loan is your collateral. Real estate, automobiles, stocks and bonds, and other valuable possessions are considered collateral. The bank has no desire to own your assets but certainly wants to know that there is something of value for the bank to collect if you default on your mortgage loan.

If your standing in each of these areas is sufficient to meet the bank's standards, you are likely to have little problem in getting approved for the loan you seek. There is, however, one additional factor over which you, unfortunately, have no control:

Conditions These are the external factors such as the national economy and local business and real estate climate that the bank may take into account in reviewing your request. These external conditions do have an impact on mortgage loans. Though we would like to believe that such broad economic conditions have little to do with our ability to meet our obligations, if the economy seems headed toward a recession, many bankers become so cautious that they won't lend you a dime. Residential mortgage requests are particularly vulnerable to general economic conditions.

☐   **THE DOWN PAYMENT**

Suppose you have saved a sum of money over a period of time at an interest rate of 5 to 8 percent. Real estate values, however, appreciated significantly over the past two decades (up to as much as 20 percent per year in some areas). No matter how much you saved, you may not have been able to keep up with inflation and rapid appreciation, and so may be as far from having your down payment as when you started saving for it. In effect, you may have been closed out of the real estate market.

The above situation, experienced by millions of potential home buyers nationally, has led to a prolonged period of "creative financing." Many first-time buyers seek a low- or no-interest loan from family members, or an advance on an inheritance, land contracts, equity sharing, buydowns, lease/purchase options, and other creative financing.

Land contracts (or installment contracts) This is used to sell a property where the owner does not convey the title until a substantial portion or all of the purchase price is paid by the buyer. This method is often used when the buyer does not have the purchase price in cash and has no lender.

Equity sharing   This technique involves several parties pooling their funds to purchase a home. One or more may reside in the property; others simply make the investment in anticipation of a return when the appreciated property is sold in the future. The percentage of ownership is spelled out in an agreement, which designates who pays the mortgage, makes repairs, and how the parties split tax benefits and profits upon the sale or refinancing of the property at some agreed-upon date.

Banks and other lenders enable people to pay progressively more during the life of a mortgage, on the assumption that their earning power will increase. Today, a minimum of 10 percent down is expected no matter how creative financing gets, and 20 percent down is common, though some people have been given a mortgage with as little as 5 percent down. On top of your down payment there are, of course, other costs including closing fees, real estate commissions, termite inspections, title searches, etc. Bankers now quickly reject applications with insufficient down payments.

☐   **KEY LOAN PROVISIONS**

Bankers and other lenders can increase or decrease the attractiveness of loans by altering key loan provisions. You should understand these provisions before you proceed to closing on a loan. A real estate agent, if you have one, should be able to explain the relevant ones to you.

Settlement Rights

Borrowers have the right under federal law to review prepared settlement statements, listing all payments to and by the borrower, at least 24 hours before closing.

Prepayment Penalty

If you wish to pay off your mortgage early, some loans provide for a penalty that assures the lender of at least a minimum return on its investment. Other loans let you pay off the mortgage early with no penalty. Unless you plan to stay in your house for 30 years and never refinance, you definitely want a loan without a prepayment penalty.

Owner Occupancy

Some loans require that the borrower use the property as his primary residence for a period of time. If you are planning to move, expect that you may be transferred, or are in the military, this kind of clause can spell trouble for you. If you are forced to move during a flat real estate market, you may find it to your advantage to rent the property to a tenant for a while, until prices go back up. An owner-occupancy clause will make that impossible. Read your mortgage papers carefully for the presence of such a clause; if it exists, ask that it be removed.

Call Privilege or Balloon Clause

This fine-print clause allows the lender to demand that the balance of the loan be paid off at the lender's discretion or at a predetermined date during the life of the loan. Again, read all the paperwork before you sign and if you find either of these clauses, ask that it be removed.

Loan Assumption or Due-on-Sale Clause

If you choose to sell your house, can the person to whom you want to sell take over your mortgage loan? Some banks allow this, on certain types of loans, subject to the bank's approval of the new borrower's credit. The presence or absence of this clause may affect your home's marketability. With the current high cost associated with new mortgage origination, this clause can improve the price you get for the house. If your purchaser can assume your low-rate loan, you may be able to sell it for a higher purchase price.

Before you sign a mortgage agreement, make sure that you have prepared for the worst-case scenario. Banks have learned recently that they can be badly hurt repossessing property. However, if you fail to make the payments as agreed, the financial institution can take steps to recover its investment—foreclosure. Often after three months of nonpayment, the bank will begin the process that will put the property up for sale at public auction. You should have at least three months' worth of mortgage payments in a savings account to tide you over in case of job loss, illness, or divorce.

❏ DIFFERENCES BETWEEN
FIXED-RATE AND ADJUSTABLE-RATE LOANS

Fixed-Rate Mortgages

These loans are available on 1-year, 15-year, and 30-year terms. The longer the term, the more it will cost you in interest. The interest rate, points, type of application, and origination fees can vary enormously. During the "hot" real estate market of the eighties, a consumer was likely to find lender differences worth $35 per month in payments on a $100,000 loan, or more than $12,000 in interest over the life of a 30-year loan.

During the softer market of the early nineties, interest rates have declined. A great deal of variation in loan packages remains, as lenders increase the number of points, the variety of loan terms, and their origination fees to make up for the lower interest rates.

With a fixed-rate mortgage, the interest rate and monthly payment amount stay the same throughout the term of the loan. During the earlier years most of the monthly payment will go toward paying off the interest. As the balance goes down slowly, the interest portion of the monthly payment goes down. In the later years of the mortgage, the borrower is paying off the principal at a higher rate.

For example, if you borrow $100,000 on a 30-year fixed-rate mortgage loan at 9 percent, your monthly payment, for principal and interest, will be $804.62. However, the part of your first payment going toward principal reduction will be only $54.62, rising to $59.30 by the twelfth payment, $64.86 by the twenty-fourth, $77.61 by the forty-eighth, and $84.88 by the sixtieth. This means that more than $725 of every monthly payment of $804.62 will be going toward interest until you have made nearly four years of payments. At the end of five years, after having made payments totaling $48,277.36, you will still owe $95,880.14 of your original $100,000.

If you are eligible for FHA or VA loans, you may be able to obtain a mortgage with a low down payment and find it easier to be approved. The VA offers mortgage loans with no down payment whatsoever. Any realtor should be able to help you determine if you qualify for these programs.

If you find that you do not qualify, you may have to delay your application for several months and repair your credit, pay off a car or a loan, or come up with a larger down payment through equity sharing or from family members. You are better off waiting until your application will be successful than risking rejection, which may sour your relationship with that lender, as well as waste time and incur expenses such as loan application fees, credit reports, and inspections.

Adjustable-Rate Mortgages (ARM)

With an ARM, your interest rate is adjusted periodically to reflect changes in market interest rates. Your loan rate fluctuates by a prearranged standard, such as the prime rate, the treasury index, or the "cost-of-funds." Comparison shopping for an ARM requires that you look at much more information than you would with a fixed-rate loan. You need to know how often the bank can

HOME LOANS

	Adjustable-Rate Mortgages	Fixed-Rate Mortgages
Rates	Rates and payments change periodically	Fixed rates and payments for loan duration
Down payment	Generally 10 to 20 percent	Generally 20 percent but can be as low as 5 percent
Advantages	Facilitates securing a larger amount Lower initial rates than fixed-rate mortgage	Constant monthly payment
Features to look for	No negative amortization Assumable to qualified buyer	No prepayment penalty

change your rate, the maximum adjustment in interest rate that will be allowed during each time period, the total adjustment that can be made over the term of the loan, and how those adjustments will be made. An initial rate that sounds reasonable may be no bargain if you end up paying more than you would have with a fixed-rate mortgage or if you are later forced to pay an amount you simply cannot afford. See the box on pages 110–112 for a review of ARM terminology.

If you are planning to be in a house for the short term, say three years, with a stable economy, you may be better off with an adjustable-rate mortgage, where the interest rate would be lower than the best fixed-rate you could possibly find.

For example, if you intend to live in a home for only three years and the ARM you are offered has an initial rate 2 points lower than a fixed-rate mortgage and can only adjust upward by a small margin each year, the ARM may be the better buy. If you plan a longer stay and want to know what your mortgage payments will be 5, 10, or 20 years from now, the fixed-rate mortgage may be for you.

Averaged nationally, mortgages are held for only seven years. Some people simply do not want to deal with fluctuation; others are willing and able to assume the risk of fluctuating payments to buy the house they want. Until you have paid off the loan and the financial history of that period is written, you will not know for sure which kind of mortgage will cost you less.

Current information and mortgage rates are offered by individual lenders and are often published in local newspapers. You can obtain educational information by writing:

Office of Thrift Supervision
Department of the Treasury
1700 G Street, N.W.
Washington, DC 20552
202-906-6000
202-906-6677

☐ SHOPPING FOR A MORTGAGE LOAN

Once you understand the choices available to you and have an amount and a property in mind, you can begin to shop for rates. The real estate section of most metropolitan newspapers carries a listing of the mortgages available from lenders in that area, including rates for fixed mortgages and ARMs. You can also call a number of area banks and mortgage companies and discuss the points, interest rates, and terms available. Keep a running log of the information you collect, noting:

Name, address, and telephone number of financial institution
Name of mortgage loan officer
Types of loans available
    conventional
        fixed-rate
        adjustable-rate
    FHA
    VA
Initiation fees

FIXED-RATE
Rate, _____ percent with _____ points, 15 years
Rate, _____ percent with _____ points, 30 years

ADJUSTABLE-RATE
Initial rate, _____ percent with _____ points
Caps: Annual _____ lifetime _____
Margin:
Index used to determine rate:

Time the bank takes to approve the loan:
    Can I lock in by telephone?
    Does the loan officer have the authority?

ARM TERMINOLOGY

ADVERTISED RATE

Usually very low (several points below the current fixed rate). Called the *initial* rate, or *teaser* rate, the loan begins at this percentage and is fixed for a short period of time, usually 6 to 12 months.

BASE RATE

The interest rate upon which your lifetime cap is calculated. Note that the base rate is not your initial rate. The base rate is very important to the total cost that you will be paying during the life of your loan.

INDEX

How your lender determines the rate of interest on your ARM. The three most commonly used are the prime rate, the Treasury index, and the cost-of-funds.

Prime Rate

Offered to the best commercial customers of a financial institution. Since so many loans hinge on this rate, any change is front-page news, and most banks adjust their prime to be competitive. Smaller banks sometimes offer a different prime from the money-center rate quoted in *The Wall Street Journal*.

Treasury Index

The most popular index for ARMs. It follows the interest rates offered by Treasury securities and reflects the ups and downs of international demand and flow of money. More volatile than the other indexes, the Treasury index can be a plus when interest rates are declining and a minus in periods of increasing rates.

Cost-of-Funds Index

An index of the average rate that lenders pay for deposits. Since the rates paid on savings accounts change less often than the prime or Treasury index, this index is more stable, taking more time to reflect escalating rates and protecting you against extreme fluctuations in your monthly payment. If your mortgage rate is pegged to a cost-of-funds index, ask which one your lender uses. The most common is the 11th District Cost-of-Funds (including California).

INTEREST (OR RATE) CAP

The interest cap limits the amount your interest rate (and payments) can increase during a specified period of time. There are two types of caps—periodic (usually annual) and lifetime. An annual cap limits the amount the interest rate can increase from one year to the next. With a 1 percent cap monthly payments will not escalate out of hand. A 3 percent increase on a $120,000 loan that started out at 10 percent will up your monthly payments from $1,050 to $1,330. With an annual cap of 1 percent, your payment could not exceed $1,140 during the next year of the loan. However, that extra $280 per month could bust your budget.

A lifetime cap limits the highest rate you will be charged at any time during the term of the loan. Make sure that your loan offers a lifetime cap that you can support. Do not sign an ARM mortgage loan without one. Imagine trying to pay 25 percent on your loan. The lifetime cap will help predict the maximum amount you will be paying on the loan at any given time if interest rates soar.

Note that many institutions have protected themselves with a base rate—the lowest rate you will pay,
Continued

ARM TERMINOLOGY *(Continued)*

even if the index to which your ARM is pegged falls lower than that. If your ARM has a base rate of 6.5 percent and your lender set the lifetime cap at 10 points above base, your interest rate would never exceed 16.5 percent. At one bank, an ARM with a fixed initial rate of 8.75 percent has caps that bottom at 6.75 and top at 14.5 percent. As the economy shifts—and perhaps as the real estate market heats up—the same bank could change its initial offering to 9.5 percent with caps of 7.5 and 15.25 percent.

MARGIN

The index plus the margin is what you will pay at the start of each adjustment period. If your ARM is based on the Treasury bills rate on a certain date, and if the rate on that date is 7.2 percent and your margin is 3 percentage points, then you will have to pay 10.2 percent on your loan for the following year.

Can I send the loan application?
Can I make an appointment to discuss this?

Amount I qualify for: _____

Check the rates quoted for you against the national rates or those from your real estate agent. Mortgage lenders get the changing rates into the hands of real estate agents immediately, usually within 24 hours of any reported change.

FIXED-RATE VERSUS ARM LOAN FOR $100,000 FOR 30 YEARS

Fixed, 9.25 percent

ARM, initial rate of 6.75 percent, with 4.75 and 12.75 percent caps

Annual payment:
$9,950.14

Payment first year:
$7,857.22

Payment every year:
$9,950.14

Annual payment possibilities: $6,320.95 (at 6.75 percent on initial balance) to $13,108.13 (at 12.75 percent on initial balance)

Each interest point above 9.25 percent would add about $848 per year or $71 per month to your payments.

Try to Negotiate Points or Initiation Fees

In a slow market, lenders may be willing to negotiate. If the rates at one bank are significantly lower than at others, check the number of points and origination fees. Ask if the bank can offer point reductions or eliminate some origination fees. Make sure you are not paying more than is standard. One single point on a $150,000 loan is $1,500.

After you have found the institution and person you can work with and are happy with the terms, ask if you can "lock in" at the quoted rate. Or, if it is higher than you want, and you are fairly confident that rates will soon go lower, you can wait to lock in at a lower fixed rate. If interest rates rise, you have lost, but if they fall, you can save thousands of dollars. This is a gamble, since interest rates change weekly and even a 1 percent increase can add up to thousands of dollars over the course of the loan. For instance, on a $100,000, 30-year fixed-rate mortgage, payments would be $877.58 at 10 percent and $952.33 at 11 percent. Over 30 years, this would add up to the difference between paying $315,929 and $342,839, or $26,910.

If you can make a sizable cash down payment, the bank may make the application process a bit easier for you. The bank may not demand a mountain of documentation about your earnings, unless you have something derogatory in your credit history.

Do Not Shortchange Your Reading and Writing

As discussed previously, request copies of loan forms. When you receive them from the bank, take time to sit down, read, and review them. Complete them precisely. Attach any supplementary data the bank wants, such as your personal financial statement, copies of pay stubs, etc.

Make an appointment with your mortgage banker and have him or her review the paperwork. That way, if there is an error, it will not be weeks before the bank gets back to you for a correction, possibly causing you to lose the chance to buy the house you really want. If the banker resists going over the forms with you, explain that you would prefer to work with his or her bank, but you cannot take a chance on losing this house.

He or she may also offer you a better deal to keep you from shopping around. Any offers made at this time should be put in writing. For example, if the officer promises to "lock" the current rate, you should get a written lock-in agreement that states the rate and the time period the lender is going to keep that rate locked. Note any other promises on your application in pen with the banker's signature and date. This addendum to the application will protect you if the bank reneges on one of its promises.

Always remember, bankers and realtors are in the business of making sales. You are the buyer, and especially when it comes to home mortgages, make sure you are getting a competitive deal.

After your loan application is in, there are several steps you can take to expedite the processing.

1. If you work at a local firm, you can have your employer write a brief note to your loan officer recommending you for the mortgage.
2. If you have a relationship with a trustee or a member of the bank's board of directors, have that person recommend you for the loan as well.
3. Call your banker every few days to see how the loan application is progressing.

Although the loan process varies, you might expect an answer within two weeks. If not, you are entitled to intervene by calling or showing up at the bank on a daily basis. Your realtor may be able to apply pressure since he or she is probably a regular source of mortgage business for the bank.

❑ YOUR LOAN HAS BEEN APPROVED

Once your loan application has been approved, you have to sign a document promising to repay the loan and an agreed-upon amount of interest. This is called a first mortgage. The "first" refers to the fact that if you do not repay the loan, your lender is first in line to take over your property. In some states it is referred to as a deed of trust or trust deed. Many mortgage agreements spell out the process if you miss payments, and some reserve the right to recall the loan if payments are late. If you fail to make your payments as agreed, the financial institution can take action to recover its investment. The "first" mortgage holder gets the total amount due after the forced sale of the property, assuming that the price is high enough. Any excess goes to second mortgage holders and other creditors.

If Your Application Is Rejected

If you have otherwise met all the criteria for getting a loan but are still turned down, you have the right to an explanation. Ask specifically for the reason the loan has been denied. In some cases, the refusal is justified, based on something you overlooked. In others, it may be a mistake on your credit report, a math error, or a bookkeeping problem. You are entitled to know exactly why.

❏ PAY YOUR MORTGAGE FIRST

Although you have other monthly obligations, the mortgage is the one bill you should pay first and always—even if you must delay other payments. Pay your mortgage on or before the date due to assure excellent credit. You have several weeks' "grace" before a penalty is imposed, but payments made two weeks after the initial due date will affect the reduction of the principal.

Should you ever be unable to make a mortgage payment on time, call your banker and ask whether the bank will accept a reduced payment for a period of time. He or she would prefer to work with you through your financial difficulty because foreclosure is an expensive, time-consuming, and messy business. If you agree to any payment agreement, follow it to the letter.

Never Walk Away

If you are caught in a desperate situation, do not walk away from your mortgage. It will ruin your credit rating for years, and since banks consider a mortgage loan among the safest they can make, it will raise questions about your reliability in all financial matters. If you have encountered a grave financial problem, most lenders, even if begrudgingly, will try to help you work it out.

❏ PREPAYMENTS

If your loan agreement allows for accelerated payment without penalty, you can save yourself thousands of dollars by exceeding the amount due monthly on the bank's payment schedule, or making an extra payment every year. Although the bank would prefer that you did *not* make additional payments—it costs them money—with most mortgages, you have every right to do so. To prepay, all you need to do is notify the lender that the extra amount should go directly for repayment of the principal, not the interest. You may want to write a separate check to ensure that the lender services your loan properly. Keep track of how much extra principal you have paid, and compare your figures with the year-end statement issued by your mortgage holder.

The prepayment reduces the amount of outstanding principal, which in turn reduces the amount of interest you would have to pay in the long run. (Some mortgages impose prepayment penalties. Review your mortgage contract or ask your lender if you are subject to any such penalties.)

Of course, you should not prepay your mortgage if you can earn more by investing the extra money elsewhere. Prepaying does not make sense if your mortgage's interest rate is lower than the yield you can earn in other investments.

Even taking into account the lost tax deductions and the lost income the extra payments could have earned in other investments, you are still likely to come out ahead by paying off your loan early.

Once you understand how much of your scheduled payment goes to interest in the early years you can see the advantage of paying more than the minimum amount. For example, if you have a fixed-rate mortgage of $100,000 at 9 percent for 30 years, and you find that you can pay about $50 extra per month, your mortgage will be paid off in approximately 23 years. An accelerated payment of $50 per month will equal about $13,800 and save you almost $53,788.30 in interest.

If you are planning to sell your property sometime over the next three to five years, however, it may be in your best interest to make only the normal monthly payment.

7

Rethinking Your Current Banking Services: Are You Getting Enough?

BEFORE DEREGULATION, BANKING WAS SIMPLER. ALL BANKS offered similar services and the government determined rates. New accounts were lured in the door with a free toaster or the choice of plain or floral checks. Now, banks are in competition with savings-and-loan institutions and credit unions for the investor's dollar. Even nationally known brokerage houses are providing services previously offered only by commercial banks. The trend seems clear; we are headed toward national banking. The giants of the banking industry are moving from state to state, scooping up business once relegated to locally based banks.

As interstate and regional banking continues to extend its domination, neither the Congress nor the courts have stepped in to stop it. Banks themselves are encouraging customers to invest in and nurture long-disance relationships, by offering money-market accounts and certificates of deposit at higher rates. The more competition and pressure banks face, the higher your potential for getting the services you want with low or no fees.

❏ CHARTING YOUR OWN MONEY HABITS

Though it's a bit rigorous, the first step in negotiating the no-cost or low-cost services you want is to analyze your banking habits. To do this, you will need to round up all of last year's bank records (from all institutions), including each month's checking and savings statements, IRA reports, and CD and other transaction summaries.

With last year's records in hand, answer the following questions:

❏   ❏   ❏

CHECKING

Approximately how many checks do you write
each month?   _____
Can that number be reduced?   Y___ N___
What was your average daily balance?   _____
What was your average minimum balance?   _____
Do you have a negotiated order of withdrawal (NOW)
account?   _____
If yes, what was the interest rate paid during the year? _____
What is the minimum amount required for free
checking?   _____
How many months did you pay a service fee?   _____
What was the annual total fee?   _____
Did you overdraw your account?   _____
How many times? _____   At what cost? _____
What was the total annual service fee?   _____

SAVINGS

What was the average monthly balance in
your savings?   _____
What was the rate of interest paid?   _____
What was the total interest paid for the year?   _____

CERTIFICATES OF DEPOSIT

Certificate of Deposit 1

Interest rate paid _____
Maturity date _____
Penalty for early _____
withdrawal

Certificate of Deposit 2

Interest rate paid _____
Maturity date _____
Penalty for early _____
withdrawal

Certificate of Deposit 3

Interest rate paid _____
Maturity date _____
Penalty for early _____
withdrawal

MISCELLANEOUS BANK SERVICES

Do you have a safe deposit box? _____
How many cashier's checks or money orders did you
  purchase this year? _____
At what cost per check? _____
Do you have a line of credit on your checking account? _____
What did you pay for traveler's checks last year? _____
What is the annual fee on your bank credit card? _____
What is the annual rate of interest charged? _____
Do you have an ATM card? If so, what were the fees
  charged for the use of that card last year? _____
Do you have overdraft protection? _____ At what
  rate of interest? _____
What amount was transferred in the past year? _____
What does your bank charge for stop-payment orders? _____
What does your bank charge for electronic transfers? _____
What did you pay last year for these services in total? _____
Do you have other loans at your bank? _____
What kind and at what rate of interest? _____
Do you use other bank services? _____
Discount brokerage services _____

Trust department   ____

Financial planning   ____

What is your total liquid net worth (cash available)?   ____

What amount is invested at your current bank?   ____

Once you have written this all on paper, you will have a much more comprehensive view of how you have been using banks, what your needs are, and what to ask for if you renegotiate the terms of your account or begin comparison shopping at other institutions.

As an additional exercise, add up the gross amount you *deposit* to your checking, savings, and investment accounts.

Next, collect competitive data. Write or call several banks that you suspect may offer the extras you seek. Clip bank advertisements that you see in newspapers and save banking-related direct-mail solicitations you receive. On a per-institution basis, use the answers to the questions above to see how different institutions compare.

Now you are armed with enough facts and figures to make the best decisions for yourself.

☐   **REVISIT YOUR BANKER**

Tell your banker that this year you would like to deposit X amount of dollars—give the total amount of last year's deposits plus whatever you currently have in savings, CDs, or IRAs.

Seek a no-charge safe deposit box. Ask for other no-charge items as your financial planning dictates. If you will need a car loan in six months, ask now for a point below the going rate. If you do a significant amount of traveling, ask for no-fee traveler's checks.

Using the information about what a competitive bank is offering, you can try to effect change at your current bank. If you cannot get the services you want, go to the other institution and use the same approach. One customer was able to get a half point off on a home mortgage, an automatic line of credit on checking, and a standing invitation to arrange appointments for her banking transactions.

When you do find a banker who will work with you, get the promises in writing before opening any accounts. Ask the banker to assist you personally in opening your accounts so you can be certain you won't have undue charges on your monthly statement.

☐ **PROBLEMS BANKS CAN SOLVE**

Beyond what you want and know to ask for, there are still other services that may be available to you at your bank. Banks provide free services to people every day. These services may or may not be advertised or listed in their brochures. But if you ask a group of bankers about the oddest job-related services they provide, the answers may range from delivering a check on New Year's eve to finding a runaway relative through financial activity in another state.

One customer had underpaid his taxes and asked for an unsecured personal loan to pay the IRS. The bank offered a 90-day personal note and the taxpayer paid both the IRS and the bank on time. If you have a problem connected to your finances—even if it's your mistake—your bank is the first place to go to seek assistance.

Especially if you have a steady, ongoing relationship with the institution, banks will often meet special customer needs such as:

- ◻ Preventing a check from bouncing
- ◻ Protecting your credit
- ◻ Informing you about whether a check written to you is "good"
- ◻ Cutting red tape in wiring money
- ◻ Providing emergency funds
- ◻ Setting up accounts for your children
- ◻ Making same-day bill payments

□ Issuing reports to your credit bureau at your request
□ Balancing your checkbook
□ Providing notary services
□ Researching and photocopying "lost" checks
□ Preparing for a financial upset
□ Working on collections
□ Serving as executor to your estate
□ Assisting in debt management

Preventing a check from bouncing If you discover a math error or have written a bad check inadvertently, see your personal banker immediately. Tell him or her the amount of the error, the date of the check, and to whom the check is written. If the banker can move "cash" from one account to another, the money will instantly clear your account and save you the risk of bouncing a check.

If you do not have the cash to move, ask the banker to give you a seven-day note on your paycheck, Social Security check, or other regular deposit. The banker has the power to cover your checks, but expect to pay interest.

Protecting your credit If a bank fails to credit a deposit or through some other error returns your check, ask the bank to write a letter explaining the error to your creditor. Also ask it to refund any fees or service charges that resulted from the erroneous return.

Informing you about whether a check written to you is "good" If you have a check from a questionable source or in an unusually large denomination, your banker will make a local call and find out if there are sufficient funds to cover the check. The bank does not want to do the paperwork associated with any "NSF" (insufficient funds) check, so it is beneficial to you both. If the check you have received is from out of town, you can call the bank it is written on, and that bank will tell you if the check will clear, provided you give it the specifics of the situation. That bank will not tell you how much is in the account.

The money you are inquiring about may have been deposited, but if it has not cleared the holding period, you could be told that there are insufficient funds in the account in question. In that case, ask when you can call back to confirm that the funds are available.

Cutting red tape in wiring money Instead of using costly commercial services or high-interest bank card advances for moving money in an emergency, you can ask your bank to put its own system of wiring money to work for you. Explain why the transaction is necessary and either for free or for a small fee, your money can be transferred from one account to another anywhere in the country, the same day. Your son in Utah, for example, can have cash available from his bank account the same day your banker wires it from yours. Make sure you provide the correct account numbers because banks wire money according to numbers, not names.

Setting up accounts for your children If your daughter is spending her junior year in college in France, your bank can offer extensive services to ensure that she has accounts in place before she moves there. The bank can also lay out a financial support system for her in case of an emergency.

Making same-day bill payment If you have a payment due to the Internal Revenue Service or are about to be late on a car or mortgage loan payment, banks can hire a delivery service to get your payment to the recipient on time. Depending on the area of the country where you live, courier services can charge from $10 to $30 for intercity delivery within an hour. They can also electronically transfer the payment for you—especially in an emergency.

Issuing reports to your credit bureau at your request If your credit history has some rough spots, your bank can assist in presenting a clear, current picture. For example, you might want to ask your banker to ensure that all bank card and automobile loan payments are included in your credit history. If you have a large sum at the bank, ask your banker to write a letter confirming your current solvency and good credit rating.

Balancing your checkbook If you hate working with numbers, for a small fee, usually $10 an hour, you can sit down with a bank representative and demystify your checkbook. Call the bank in advance to make an appointment. Take your checkbook and canceled checks with you. The bank will be working from a computer printout of your account. If there is an error, it can be cleared up instantly. If your checkbook is hopelessly tangled, this service will give you a fresh start and make recordkeeping easier in the future.

Providing notary services Most banks have a notary public on the premises. When a document needs to be notarized, your bank can provide the service to you at no charge.

Researching and photocopying "lost" checks Providing the IRS with proof of a charitable donation made a few years ago can be an arduous task. Your bank can help. For a small fee, about $3, it will provide a notarized "copy" of the check from its microfiche records. This service is also useful in court to prove you made payments.

Preparing for a financial upset For example, if you suspect that your spouse is about to institute divorce proceedings and might try to take sole physical possession of your joint assets, your banker can arrange to have your accounts "monitored" for large withdrawals by the cosigner or, with the spouse's agreement, you can have the accounts changed to require both parties' signatures for withdrawals.

You can also have accounts tagged "POD" (payable on death) so that if a party dies, the money is immediately available to the other account holder and does not get locked in probate. Other sensitive services are also available, and for the most part, bankers will respect your privacy in these matters. Inform your banker of your situation and ask what you can do legally to protect yourself.

Working on collections If you are a landlord, receive court-decreed child support, or have other business that requires regular payment, you can arrange to have the payment made directly to the bank. If a payment is late, you can enlist the bank's collections department to write the letter or make necessary telephone calls. Private collection agencies charge a percentage of what they recover; your bank will not. Banks also have legal departments or attorneys on retainer that will go to work on collections for you—either at no charge or at a far lower fee than you would pay elsewhere.

Serving as executor to your estate Many adult children do not reside in the same town as their parents. This makes managing personal affairs after the death of a parent more difficult. Your banker can serve as the coexecutor for your estate, taking care of your local affairs with the supervision of the individual whom you have named as the other coexecutor, be it your other parent, sister, or best friend.

Larger banks have trust departments for estate planning. Smaller banks offer similar services, but on a more personal basis. Some bankers will keep a copy of your will on file.

Assisting in debt management If your business fails or you lose your job, you may find yourself strapped financially. A banker can serve as your ally in making arrangements with your creditors to help you get back on your feet.

For example, if you have been a long-term good customer, your banker may be able to offer a debt-consolidation loan to reduce your present payments.

❑   **OTHER SPECIAL SERVICES**

Your bank can also help you plan for retirement, reduce the amount you pay in taxes, send your child to college, or select high-yield investments. Banks now offer money-management services such as financial planning, estate planning, investor services, and other forms of consulting advice at no charge to their customers.

However, bank professionals pass no test or certification procedure to qualify them for dispensing such services, so be sure to ask about your banker's background in financial planning, as well as his or her performance record, in addition to references from long-term customers.

☐ **ESTATE PLANNING WITH YOUR BANKER**

Most banks offer estate planning services to their customers, services that most people never use, much less know about. Estate planning can seem intimidating because it has a language all its own, but it is no more complex than buying a home, car, or paying your income tax. Basically, an *estate* consists of the things you own and the cash you have on hand, which becomes a legal entity after you die. In the event of your death, estate planning simplifies and reduces the costs of the legal process as well as the amount of estate taxes paid to the federal, state, and local governments. It ensures that your assets go to the heirs you have named.

Many customers assume that their estates are too small to discuss with an estate planner. And yet, with the average value of homes escalating annually, along with the cost of cars, boats, jewelry, and even household furnishings, your total net worth is probably higher than you think. You can tap your bank for key advice on protecting what you have.

Experts recommend that you begin thinking about estate planning when you get married and certainly when you have children, and that every few years, as your assets grow, you should update your plan.

Ask Your Banker About Wills

A *will* is the legal document that describes how you direct your estate to be dissolved and distributed. Many successful professionals do not have one, erroneously believing that when they die, their spouse will simply inherit everything. Depending on the state where you live, if you die without leaving a will, the federal and state governments could take as much as a third of what you have, giving half of it to your children, and for years tie up in probate what money remains.

Your banker can be an invaluable resource to prevent this from happening to your family. He or she can help you convert your checking and savings accounts to ones with rights of joint survivorship, create POD (payable-on-death) accounts, arrange for heirs to have access to your safe deposit box, and suggest an attorney to draw up the papers.

Probate is the legal process of validating your will, making an inventory of your assets, paying estate taxes, and dispersing the assets among those you have named to receive them, called *heirs* or *beneficiaries*. An asset or gift bestowed is called a *bequest*. *Distribution* is simply who gets what. If your estate planner also serves as manager, he is called an *executor*, if male, or an *executrix*, if female. If you have children, you will be asked who should be appointed *guardian* to raise your children should you die while they are still minors.

Taxes, Gifts, and Trusts

Much of your estate planning will include a discussion about *taxes*, since there may be estate taxes, inheritance taxes, and income taxes to be paid when you die. The marital-deduction clause in the Federal Tax Code allows you to leave as much as you want to your spouse tax-free; you can do this for other heirs tax-free as well. This is not, however, a do-it-yourself process. Each state has different laws regarding estate taxes, and a mistake can cost your family your fortune.

Ask your banker about federal regulations regarding the gift tax, which allows you to make gifts up to $10,000 each year to each beneficiary. If you pass on your money to children and grandchildren as a *gift*, they will get a large portion of it tax-free, although the person giving it still faces federal and state income taxes on the money if it represents income for that year.

You may be advised to create a number of *trusts*, which are ways to take money directly out of your estate at the time of your death and put it directly into the hands of those you designate. There are *living trusts*, which transfer ownership of assets before you die, and dozens of others that have particular advantages for certain situations.

After receiving advice from the trust department of your bank, review the plan with a family attorney. It will give you greater peace of mind.

ACRONYMS

The world of banking is strewn with acronyms; unless you know what they mean (see definitions in glossary), you could be at a disadvantage in making your bank work for you. If you can use them at the bank, all the better:

ARM	adjustable-rate mortgage
APR	annual percentage rate
ATM	automated teller machine
CD	certificate of deposit
EFT	electronic funds transfer
FDIC	Federal Deposit Insurance Corporation
FIRREA	Financial Institutions Reform, Recovery and Enforcement Act
IRA	Individual Retirement Account
NCUA	National Credit Union Administration

NOW	negotiated order of withdrawal
PIN	personal identification number
POD	payable on death
SAIF	Savings Association Insurance Fund
SEC	Securities and Exchange Commission

GLOSSARY

ADJUSTABLE-RATE MORTGAGE (ARM). A mortgage with interest rates that may shift periodically based on changes in a specified interest index. Initially, the rates on ARMs are usually lower than those on fixed-rate mortgages.

ANNUAL PERCENTAGE RATE (APR). The finance charge on a loan over a one-year period, expressed as a percentage. Refers to the actual cost of a loan annually, and includes the cost of any loan fees as well as credit reports. When making a borrowing decision it is best to compare APRs rather than just the fixed or adjustable rates.

APPRAISAL FEE. The charge for estimating the value of an asset.

APPRECIATION. The increase in the value of an asset above its cost or current value.

ASSET. Any item that has monetary value.

ASSUMABLE LOAN. If a loan is assumable, the seller may be able to transfer the loan to a new buyer, under the same terms and interest rate. Some loans have no limits on assumption, others can be assumed once, others not at all.

ATMs. Automated teller machines allow you to gain access to funds in your checking and combined savings accounts, and more, depending on the particular ATM system you are using.

BALANCE SHEET. An itemized statement that lists the assets, liabilities, and difference between the two, called the net worth.

BANK EXAMINER. An outside professional who verifies whether a bank's loans have been made in accordance with existing guidelines, policies, and procedures.

CASH FLOW. The difference between cash receipts and disbursements over a given period of time. The clearest measure of liquidity.

CD. A certificate of deposit, also called a time deposit. Short-term maturities range from 76 to 364 days; long-term from 1 to 15 years.

COLLATERAL. An asset pledged to a creditor to ensure repayment of a debt. When repayment is not made in a timely manner, the lender may seize and sell the collateral to retire the obligation.

COMMERCIAL BANK. A federal- or state-chartered corporation that provides a range of banking services.

COMMERCIAL LOAN. A loan made to a business.

COMMISSION. The fee charged by a broker for executing the purchase or sale of securities.

CONSOLIDATION LOAN. A loan that consolidates several debts into a single loan.

CREDIT. An agreement to receive money, goods, or services now, and to pay for them in the future. With bank loans, the bank is the creditor and the borrower is the debtor.

CREDIT BUREAU. A private agency that collects credit information on an ongoing basis from firms that grant credit and supplies such information to the bureau's membership for a fee.

CREDIT HISTORY. A record of a borrower's debts and payment habits.

CREDIT REPORT. A report compiled by a credit bureau that lists information provided by credit-granting organizations.

CREDITWORTHINESS. The ability and willingness of a person to repay his or her debts.

CURRENT ASSETS. Various forms of cash and all items owned by an individual or business that normally can be converted into cash within a year, including accounts receivable and inventory.

CURRENT LIABILITIES. Accounts payable, notes payable, the current portion of long-term debt, mortgages, and all items owed by an individual or business that are normally expected to be paid within a year.

DEFAULT. Failure to meet the payment terms of a credit agreement.

DELINQUENT LOAN. A loan where payment is past due and no other arrangements have been made with the bank.

DEPRECIATION. An adjustment to the bookkeeping value of an asset that theoretically reflects its declining value.

EQUITY. See HOME EQUITY, also NET WORTH.

FEDERAL DEPOSIT INSURANCE CORPORATION. A government corporation that insures most bank and savings-and-loan deposits.

FINANCE CHARGES. The cost of a loan in actual dollars and cents, as required by the federal Truth-in-Lending Act of 1968.

FIXED ASSETS. Assets that normally will not be converted into cash during the coming year, such as plant equipment.

HOME EQUITY. The difference between the value of your home and what is owed on your mortgage.

INDIVIDUAL RETIREMENT ACCOUNT. A tax-deferred account established under Section 408(a) of the Internal Revenue Code to provide for one's retirement, and, after death, the support of one's beneficiaries.

LIABILITIES. Any item of value that is owed by an individual or a company.

LINE OF CREDIT. An agreement whereby the bank makes available a sum of money with an upper limit that can be drawn upon by a borrower who has frequent borrowing needs. A line of credit is considered a loan.

LOAN OFFICER. A bank officer with the responsibility of approving and declining loan applications.

LONG-TERM DEBT. An obligation not due within the next year, such as the long-term portion of a loan, excluding your current monthly payments.

MONEY-CENTER BANKS. The largest banks in the United States, which traditionally have dominated the banking industry.

MORTGAGE. A loan with property pledged as collateral.

NET WORTH. The difference between total assets and total liabilities.

OVERDRAFT. A negative balance in your checking account as a result of more money being taken out than is available in the account.

PERSONAL FINANCIAL STATEMENT. An individual's listing of personal assets, liabilities, and net worth as of a given date.

PIN. A personal identification number code that enables cardholders to use automated teller machines.

POINTS. A fee charged by a lender. Points are equal to 1 percent of the loan's principal.

PRIME RATE. The rate of interest that banks charge their most creditworthy business customers.

PRINCIPAL. The amount you borrow, not including interest, finance charges, or other loan expenses. It is referred to as the outstanding balance at the outset of the loan.

SECOND MORTGAGE. A second loan secured by the equity in your home or vacation home, sometimes called a home-equity loan.

SECURED LOAN. A loan with an asset pledged as collateral.

UNSECURED LOAN. A loan made without collateral required.

YIELD. The amount investments actually earn, which varies according to how the interest is compounded. Yields are higher with daily compounding than with monthly, quarterly, or annual compounding.

INDEX